THE POWER OF LOVE

THE STUDY OF 1 CORINTHIANS 13

DR. DAVID JEREMIAH

with Dr. David Jeremiah

CONTENTS

About
Dr. David Jeremiah
and Turning Point

D r. David Jeremiah is the founder of Turning Point, a ministry committed to providing Christians with sound Bible teaching relevant to today's changing times through radio and television broadcasts, audio series, books, and live events. Dr. Jeremiah's common-sense teaching on topics such as family, prayer, worship, angels, and biblical prophecy forms the foundation of Turning Point.

David and his wife, Donna, reside in El Cajon, California, where he serves as the senior pastor of Shadow Mountain Community Church. David and Donna have four children and twelve grandchildren.

In 1982, Dr. Jeremiah brought the same solid teaching to San Diego television that he shares weekly with his congregation. Shortly thereafter, Turning Point expanded its ministry to radio. Dr. Jeremiah's inspiring messages can now be heard worldwide on radio, television, and the Internet.

Because Dr. Jeremiah desires to know his listening audience, he travels nationwide holding ministry rallies that touch the hearts and lives of many people. According to Dr. Jeremiah, "At some point in time, everyone reaches a turning point; and for every person, that moment is unique, an experience to hold onto forever. There's so much changing in today's world that sometimes it's difficult to choose the right path. Turning Point offers people an understanding of God's Word as well as the opportunity to make a difference in their lives."

Dr. Jeremiah has authored numerous books, including *Escape the Coming Night* (Revelation), *The Handwriting on the Wall* (Daniel), *Overcoming Loneliness, Prayer—The Great Adventure, When Your World Falls Apart, My Heart's Desire, 31 Days to Happiness—Searching for Heaven on Earth, Signs of Life, What in the World Is Going On?, I Never Thought I'd See the Day!, What Are You Afraid Of?, Agents of the Apocalypse, RESET —Ten Steps to Spiritual Renewal, The Book of Signs, Overcomer* and *The World of the End.*

HOW TO USE THIS STUDY GUIDE

The purpose of this Turning Point study guide is to reinforce Dr. David Jeremiah's dynamic, in-depth teaching and to aid the reader in applying biblical truth to his or her daily life. This study guide is designed to be used in conjunction with Dr. Jeremiah's *The Power of Love* audio series, but it may also be used by itself for personal or group study.

STRUCTURE OF THE LESSONS

Each lesson is based on one of the messages in the *The Power of Love* compact disc series and focuses on specific passages in the Bible. Each lesson is composed of the following elements:

- *Outline*

The outline at the beginning of the lesson gives a clear, concise picture of the topic being studied and provides a helpful framework for readers as they listen to Dr. Jeremiah's teaching.

- *Overview*

The overview summarizes Dr. Jeremiah's teaching on the passage being studied in the lesson. Readers should refer to the Scripture passages in their own Bibles as they study the overview. Unless otherwise indicated, Scripture verses quoted are taken from the New King James Version.

- *Personal and Group Application Questions*

This section contains a variety of questions designed to help readers dig deeper into the lesson and the Scriptures, and to apply the lesson to their daily lives. For Bible study groups or Sunday school classes, these questions will provide a springboard for group discussion and interaction.

- *Did You Know?*

This section presents a fascinating fact, historical note, or insight that adds a point of interest to the preceding lesson.

PERSONAL STUDY

Thank you for selecting *The Power of Love* for your current study. The lessons in this study guide were created to help you gain fresh insights into God's Word and develop new perspectives on topics you may have previously studied. Each lesson is designed to challenge your thinking, and help you grow in your knowledge of Christ. During your study, it is our prayer that you will discover how biblical truth affects every aspect of your life and your relationship with Christ will be strengthened.

When you commit to completing this study guide, try to set apart a time, daily or weekly, to read through the lessons without distraction. Have your Bible nearby when you read the study guide, so you're ready to look up verses if you need to. If you want to use a notebook to write down your thoughts, be sure to have that handy as well. Take your time to think through and answer the questions. If you plan on reading the study guide with a small group, be sure to read ahead and be prepared to take part in the weekly discussions.

LEADER'S GUIDE

Thank you for your commitment to lead a group through *The Power of Love*. Being a leader has its own rewards. You may discover that your walk with the Lord deepens through this experience. Throughout the study guide, your group will explore new topics and review study questions that encourage thought-provoking group discussion.

The lessons in this study guide are suitable for Sunday school classes, small-group studies, elective Bible studies, or home Bible study groups. Each lesson is structured to provoke thought and help you grow in your knowledge and understanding of God. There are multiple components in this section that can help you structure your lessons and discussion time, so make sure you read and consider each one.

Before You Begin

Before you begin each meeting, make sure you and your group are well-versed with the content of the chapter. Every person should have his or her own study guide so they can follow along and write in the study guide if need be. When possible, the study guide should be used with the corresponding compact disc series. You may wish to assign the study guide lesson as homework prior to the meeting of the group and then use the meeting time to listen to the CD and discuss the lesson.

To ensure that everyone has a chance to participate in the discussion, the ideal size for a group is around eight to ten people. If there are more than ten people, try to break up the bigger group into smaller subgroups. Make sure the members are committed to participating each week, as this will help create stability and help you better prepare the structure of the meeting.

At the beginning of the study each week, start the session with a question to challenge group members to think about the issues you will be discussing. The members can answer briefly, but the goal is to have an idea in their mind as you go over the lesson. This allows the group members to become engaged and ready to interact with the group.

After reviewing the lesson, try to initiate a free-flowing discussion. Invite group members to bring questions and insights they may have discovered to the next meeting, especially if they were unsure of the meaning of some parts of the lesson. Be prepared to discuss how biblical truth applies to the world we live in today.

Weekly Preparation

As the group leader, here are a few things you can do to prepare for each meeting:

- Choose whether or not you will play the CD message during your small group session.

  If you decide to play the CD message from Dr. Jeremiah as part of the meeting, you will need to adjust the group time accordingly.

- Make sure you are thoroughly familiar with the material in the lesson.

  Make sure you understand the content of the lesson so you know how to structure group time and you are prepared to lead group discussion.

- Decide, ahead of time, which questions you plan to discuss.

  Depending on how much time you have each week, you may not be able to reflect on every question. Select specific questions which you feel will evoke the best discussion.

- Take prayer requests.

  At the end of your discussion, take prayer requests from your group members and pray for each other.

Structuring the Discussion Time

If you need help in organizing your time when planning your group Bible study, here are two schedules, for sixty minutes and ninety minutes, which can give you a structure for the lesson:

Option 1 (Listen to Audio CD)	60 Minutes	90 Minutes
Welcome: Members arrive and get settled.	N/A	5 minutes
Getting Started Question: Prepares the group for interacting with one another.	Welcome and Getting Started 5 minutes	15 minutes
Message: Listen to the audio CD.	40 minutes	40 minutes
Discussion: Discuss group study questions.	10 minutes	25 minutes
Prayer and Application: Final application for the week and prayer before dismissal.	5 minutes	5 minutes

Option 2 (No Audio CD)	60 Minutes	90 Minutes
Welcome: Members arrive and get settled.	5 minutes	10 minutes
Getting Started Question: Prepares the group for interacting with one another.	10 minutes	10 minutes
Message: Review the lesson.	15 minutes	25 minutes
Discussion: Discuss group study questions.	25 minutes	35 minutes
Prayer and Application: Final application for the week and prayer before dismissal.	5 minutes	10 minutes

As the group leader, it is up to you to keep track of the time and keep things moving along according to your schedule. If your group is having a good discussion, don't feel the need to stop and move on to the next question. Remember, the purpose is to pull together ideas, and share unique insights on the lesson. Make time each week to discuss how to apply these truths to living for Christ today.

The purpose of discussion is for everyone to participate, but don't be concerned if certain group members are more quiet—they may be internally reflecting on the questions and need time to process their ideas before they can share them.

Group Dynamics

Leading a group study can be a rewarding experience for you and your group members—but that doesn't mean there won't be challenges. Certain members may feel uncomfortable discussing topics that they consider very personal, and might be afraid of being called on. Some members might have disagreements on specific issues. To help prevent these scenarios, consider the following ground rules:

- If someone has a question that may seem off topic, suggest that it is discussed at another time, or ask the group if they are okay with addressing that topic.

- If someone asks a question you don't know the answer to, confess that you don't know and move on. If you feel comfortable, invite other group members to give their opinions, or share their comments based on personal experience.

- If you feel like a couple of people are talking much more than others, direct questions to people who may not have shared yet. You could even ask the more dominating members to help draw out the quiet ones.

- When there is a disagreement, encourage the group members to process the matter in love. Invite members from opposing sides to evaluate their opinions and consider the ideas of the other members. Lead the group through Scripture that addresses the topic, and look for common ground.

When issues arise, remind your group to think of Scripture: "Love one another" (John 13:34), "If it is possible, as much as depends on you, live peaceably with all men" (Romans 12:18), and "Be quick to listen, slow to speak and slow to become angry" (James 1:19, NIV).

For Continuing Study

For a complete listing of Dr. Jeremiah's materials for personal and group study call 1-800-947-1993, go online to www.DavidJeremiah.org, or write to Turning Point, P.O. Box 3838, San Diego, CA 92163.

Dr. Jeremiah's *Turning Point* program is currently heard or viewed around the world on radio, television, and the Internet in English. *Momento Decisivo,* the Spanish translation of Dr. Jeremiah's messages, can be heard on radio in every Spanish speaking country in the world. The television broadcast is also broadcast by satellite throughout the Middle East with Arabic subtitles.

Contact Turning Point for radio and television program times and stations in your area, or visit our website at www.DavidJeremiah.org/stationlocator.

THE POWER OF LOVE

J. Allan Peterson, in his book *The Myth of the Greener Grass*, tells a fascinating story of the power of love.

A woman came into the office of a minister named George Crane to talk about how much she hated her husband. "I do not only want to get rid of him," she said, "I want to get even. But before I divorce him, I want to hurt him as much as he has hurt me."

Dr. Crane came up with an ingenious plan to help the woman achieve her goal—or so she thought: "Go home and act as if you really love your husband. Tell him how much he means to you. Praise him for every good and decent trait you think he has. Go out of your way to be as kind, considerate, and generous as possible. Spare no efforts to please him and to enjoy him. Make him believe you love him. After you've convinced him of your undying love and that you cannot live without him, then drop the bomb! Tell him you're getting a divorce. That will really hurt him, and you'll achieve your goal."

"Beautiful!" the woman said with a devious smile and revenge in her eyes. "He'll be totally surprised."

So the woman followed Dr. Crane's "prescription for revenge and divorce" to the letter. For two months she acted as if she was totally in love with her husband. She loved, listened, gave, encouraged, supported, and did it all expecting nothing in return. She acted like a person who was head over heels in love.

After Dr. Crane failed to hear from the woman after a couple of months, he called her up and asked how things had gone; if she was ready to go through with the divorce. "Divorce?" the woman exclaimed. "Never! I discovered I really do love him!"

The interesting thing about this story is that the woman entered into her plan with hateful feelings toward her husband. Yet two months later, her feelings had changed completely. The only thing that changed was her behavior—she practiced loving actions and attitudes in spite of how she felt. She proved the biblical teaching that love is most accurately communicated by actions, not by feelings.

Too often people measure their love by how they feel. The woman in the story, along with countless other men and women every day, conclude they don't love their spouses any more because they don't feel like they're in love. When we say we don't love someone, what we're really saying is that we have chosen not to practice loving acts and attitudes toward that person. Because love, according to 1 Corinthians 13, is best viewed as a verb (something we do), not a noun (something that exists).

Take John 3:16 as an example: "For God so loved the world that He *gave* His only begotten Son" (emphasis added). God demonstrated His love by an action—by giving. We could provide a number of other verbs by which God "so loved the world": He forgave, He reconciled, He blessed, He gave, He justified, He sanctified—and on and on. Nowhere does the Bible say, "For God so loved the word that He *felt*."

The power of love is bound up in its actions—its choices, day in and day out, to seek the very best for another person without the expectation of anything in return. And this study guide, *The Power of Love,* is written to explain those choices as listed by the apostle Paul in 1 Corinthians 13.

These choices (behaviors and attitudes) will bring the power of love to bear on every human relationship, and they are guaranteed. For as Paul wrote in verse 8 of his chapter on love, "Love never fails."

THE POWER AND PRIORITY OF LOVE

1 Corinthians 13:1-3

In this lesson we are introduced to the preeminent attribute of God and those who know Him: love.

OUTLINE

Ask a hundred people on the street to define love, and you'll get a hundred different answers. Some will even spell it "luv" to give it a warm and fuzzy vibe. While the Bible doesn't define love, it definitely personifies and illustrates it. God is love—and so should His followers be.

I. **The Priority of Love**
   A. Love Is the Priority Commandment
   B. Love Is the Perfect Gift
   C. Love Is the Preeminent Grace
   D. Love Is the Permanent Virtue
   E. Love Is the Proof of Our Sonship
   F. Love Is the Prerequisite of Faith
   G. Love Is the Path Upon Which Christians Must Walk
   H. Love Is the Prescription for Happy Homes

II. **The Passage About Love**
   A. Precise in Its Presentation
   B. Problematic in Its Context

III. **The Preeminence of Love**
   A. Words Without Love Are Nothing
   B. I, Without Love, Am Nothing
   C. Wisdom Without Love Is Nothing

The famous book of quotations edited by John Bartlett has around thirteen hundred different definitions, reflections, and opinions on "love" by the world's great writers, thinkers, philosophers, and theologians. No wonder the world is confused about the meaning of love! The abundance of views on the subject shows that love remains the most popular and powerful emotion in the world.

In the biblical world there were four different terms, all of which could be translated by our English word *love*, but all having slightly different shades of meaning. The most common was *eros,* the word for sexual or sensual love, from which our word *erotic* springs. It is not found in the Greek New Testament.

A second word was *storge,* a word that speaks of familial love or filial love between a parent and a child. It was even used in Greek literature to describe relations between animals.

Phileo refers to psychological or social love, often translated by "friend" (John 15:13-14). It also suggests "brotherly love"—the affection shared between companions. *Phileo* and related words are found often in the New Testament.

The fourth word, *agape,* is the kind of love most associated with the New Testament. *Agape* is unconditional, divine love, the kind of love God exercises toward mankind. Indeed, 1 John 4:8 and 16 say that "God is love *[agape]."*

At the heart of *agape* is sacrifice. It is not the spontaneous, impulsive love we see on television and in the movies. It is the reasoning, esteeming, and choosing type of love. *Agape* is used almost exclusively in the writings of the New Testament because in the Greek world of the day it was such a rare idea. *Eros* dominated the pagan cultures of that time, and sacrificial, unconditional love was almost unheard of. *Agape* is the highest form of love—the love everyone wants to receive but few seem ready to give because of the sacrifice involved.

One of the best definitions of *agape* I've ever read is this: *"Agape* love is the power that moves us to respond to someone's needs with no expectation of reward." The chapter in the New Testament that Paul wrote about *agape* love, 1 Corinthians 13, illustrates that definition beautifully. Throughout the New Testament we find examples of God's love and realize that we are commanded to love just as He did: sacrificially. The core idea of *agape* love is the willingness to give oneself without reservation to another person for his or her well-being—without expectation of reward.

New Testament theologian Leon Morris has described love this way: "Agape is a new word for a new idea. Whereas the best concept of love before the New Testament was that of a love for the best that one knows, the Christian's thought of love is the quality that we see displayed in the cross. It is a love for the utterly unworthy, a love which proceeds from a God who is love. It is love lavished upon others without a thought of whether they are worthy to receive it or not. The Christian who has experienced God's love to him while he was yet a sinner has been transformed by that experience, and now he sees men everywhere as the objects of God's love, and as those for whom Christ died."[1]

As much as we think we are loving our spouse, child, friend, or coworker, it is easy to fall into the trap of expecting something in return: "No matter what I do for him/her, I get no response at all." So? *Agape* doesn't love to get a response. It loves to do good whether the loved one responds or not. No matter what the loved one does, *agape* keeps on doing good because its goal is love "in spite of," not "because of."

God's love for man is the central theme of the Bible, of course, from Genesis to Revelation—it is the priority attribute of God's relationship with man. Therefore, if we are to mirror God's actions toward us in our actions toward others, love must be our priority as well.

THE PRIORITY OF LOVE

There are eight reasons why love must be the top priority in our life.

Love Is the Priority Commandment

In Matthew 22:36-40, Jesus said that the greatest commandment was to love God, and the second greatest was to love one's neighbor —that loving God and others was a summary of all that the law and the prophets taught. Yes, He was quoting the Old Testament when He said that, but the New Testament is no less focused on the priority of love. We are told to love 55 different times in the New Testament.

Love Is the Perfect Gift

In the chapter preceding Paul's great chapter on love, the apostle had engaged the Corinthian church on the subject of spiritual gifts, the exercise of which had become unbalanced in Corinth.

He concluded that chapter with these words: "And yet I show you a more excellent way" (12:31). That way, of course, is love, his subject in 1 Corinthians 13. It is the key ingredient in the exercise of spiritual gifts, making it the perfect gift.

Love Is the Preeminent Grace

Paul states plainly in 1 Corinthians 13:13 that the "greatest" expression of God's grace is love. Nine of those expressions, including love as the first in the list, are described by Paul as the fruit of the Spirit in Galatians 5:22-23. Both Paul and Peter, in other Scriptures (Colossians 3:14; 1 Peter 4:8), affirm the preeminence of love. Because the Bible says God is love, it should come as no surprise that love is the most important manifestation of His grace.

Love Is the Permanent Virtue

There is never a time when love is inappropriate or a bad choice —it is the permanent virtue: "Love never fails" (1 Corinthians 13:8). This world is passing away (failing)—including spiritual gifts— but love never will.

Love Is the Proof of Our Sonship

Jesus told His disciples in John 13:35 that love is the brand, or mark, by which the world would recognize them as His disciples. Love is a greater evidence of our relationship with Jesus than anything we might say.

Love Is the Prerequisite of Faith

Faith does not work on its own in the Christian life—it is "faith working through love" (Galatians 5:6). "Love from a pure heart" (1 Timothy 1:5) means that love is the "setting" for all that we do in the faith life.

Love Is the Path Upon Which Christians Must Walk

Love was what characterized the words and works of Jesus Christ and what must characterize the lives of His followers. Paul wrote, "Walk in love, as Christ also has loved us" (Ephesians 5:1-2).

Love Is the Prescription for Happy Homes

Just as Jesus Christ, as the Head of the Church, loves the Church, so husbands are to love their wives in the same way (Ephesians 5:25). Husbands are given the primary responsibility for initiating and maintaining the consistency of love in the home.

There is one extended passage of Scripture that illustrates what *agape* love is like: 1 Corinthians 13.

THE PASSAGE ABOUT LOVE

Looking at 1 Corinthians 13 through two lenses—its precision and its problematic context—will help to understand Paul's words.

Precise in Its Presentation

With just 271 words, the apostle Paul penned the greatest description of love in all of world literature. His words are precise, focused, and very practical. John Wesley regarded 1 Corinthians 13 as the greatest chapter in the Bible. Nothing says what love is better than this short chapter. No one who wants to know how to love another person with *agape* love should be confused about what that means after reading Paul's words.

Problematic in Its Context

Too often, 1 Corinthians 13 is read without the benefit of its context in Paul's first letter to the Corinthians. The church at Corinth lacked none of the spiritual gifts (1 Corinthians 1:4-7), but they lacked the love necessary to make those gifts true manifestations of the grace of God. Paul spent much time in this letter correcting their attitudes, beliefs, and behaviors. His words on love come immediately between a chapter explaining spiritual gifts (chapter 12) and a chapter on exercising spiritual gifts (chapter 14). Love (chapter 13) is the bridge between belief and behavior, between position and practice.

Paul's point is that you can't exercise spiritual gifts in a carnal manner and have them represent the Giver of the gifts, the Holy Spirit. Love is the "lubricant" that makes the gears of the gifts turn smoothly in the Church. Gifts exercised without love are meaningless.

The Corinthians were exercising their gifts, but they needed to do it in a "more excellent way" (1 Corinthians 12:31). They needed to "pursue love" along with their pursuit of the gifts (1 Corinthians 14:1).

THE PREEMINENCE OF LOVE

The first section (verses 1-3) of Paul's chapter on love makes this single point: Love is preeminent over everything else. Five times in this section, Paul uses the phrase "though I"; and three times he says "have not." In other words, "though I" do this or that but "have not" love, I've missed the whole point. Love is more important than the "this or that" we think is so critical.

Words Without Love Are Nothing

Oratory is a great gift; but apart from love, our words are just so much noise ("sounding brass or a clanging cymbal," verse 1). The Greeks prided themselves on the spoken word, so this rebuke probably stung the Corinthians to the core. Carnality makes it impossible to hear a speaker's words no matter how profound. Adolf Hitler was a powerful orator who led a nation to ruin because of his hatred for non-Aryan peoples. But David Livingstone, missionary to Africa, won the hearts of native Africans in spite of his poor verbal skills—because they sensed his love for them.

LeRoy Koopman has done a modernization of this section that puts Paul's point into contemporary language: "If I speak to others with careful politeness and observe all the rules of etiquette, I am as an eight-year-old learning to play the trumpet. If I speak with the power of Billy Graham and the profundity of Harvey Cox, but have not love, I am a howling loudspeaker, or a radio with static. If I pledge eternal devotion and make thrilling professions of endearment, but have not love, I am the howling of a wolf at midnight. If I speak words of quiet sympathy and concern, but have not love, I am as soothing as an ambulance siren in the night." [2]

I, Without Love, Am Nothing

Paul focuses on the gift of prophecy in verse 2 (which he later confirms to be the greatest of the spiritual gifts—1 Corinthians 14:5). Even though it is the most important spiritual gift, if it is exercised in a carnal fashion (without love), it is "nothing." More specifically, the person who exercises the gift is nothing. Apparently the Corinthians thought they could gain spiritual stature by understanding "all mysteries and all knowledge" and by having mountain-moving faith. Not so. The person with spiritual gifts like that negates those gifts by his or her lack of love.

Wisdom Without Love Is Nothing

No matter how committed we are to teaching, to speaking, or to ministry, without love "it profits [us] nothing" (verse 3). As Paul wrote in 1 Corinthians 8:1, "Knowledge puffs up, but love edifies." If we are going to make an impact on people through our ministry —the teaching, wisdom, or counsel we offer—it will have to be couched in love. As has been so often said, "People don't care how much you know until they know how much you care."

Nor are good works—giving up everything for the poor or dying as a martyr—of any ultimate value if they are not done in a sacrificial, loving way. Many times money is given away for the purpose of getting a tax deduction. But is that evidence of love? And lots of seemingly sacrificial work is done for purposes of self-promotion. But is that love? Neither giving nor martyrdom in themselves serve their true purpose if they are not bathed in love.

It is possible, Paul writes, to accomplish seemingly wise, important, powerful, and noble works—all without love. That would make us the exact opposite of the God who is love. Everything God does is motivated by sacrificial, *agape* love. And because His Son lives in us by the presence of the Holy Spirit, all we do should be characterized by that same kind of love. Hopefully the lessons in this study guide will lead you further toward realizing the power of God's love in your life.

By studying 1 Corinthians 13, we will see how love can provide power over envy, pride, anger, discouragement, selfishness, and other carnal attitudes. When love becomes the priority in our life, nothing can overpower it.

Notes

1. Leon Morris, *First Epistle of Paul to the Corinthians: An Introduction and Commentary* (Grand Rapids: Eerdmans, 1958).

2. LeRoy Koopman, *Beauty Care for the Tongue* (Grand Rapids: Zondervan, 1974).

1. What is the greatest commandment?

2. What is the second greatest?

3. How do they tie into each other? (Matthew 22:37-39)

4. How can you follow these commands wholeheartedly?

5. What key ingredient in the exercise of spiritual gifts is referred to in 1 Corinthians 12:31?

   a. How often do you exercise the gift of love? In what ways can it be hard to exercise this gift?

   b. How would you define what it means to "pursue love"? (1 Corinthians 14:1) Do you pursue love?

6. What is the standard, or template, for how we are to love one another? (Ephesians 5:2)

   a. Is there anyone whom you struggle to love? How can you learn to embrace and see that person as a child of God?

b. In what sense does performing otherwise commendable acts without the motivation of love change the value of the act? Does any value remain? In what way?

7. How does Matthew 6:1-4 add insight to 1 Corinthians 13:1-3?

8. Name something valuable in your life. Compare giving it up with what God gave up. (1 John 4:9)

a. How can this put your priorities in perspective?

b. Based purely on the example of God's love, how would you define *sacrifice*?

c. As a Christian, why is sacrifice important?

d. What types of sacrifices are Christians called to make?

e. Describe a sacrificial act you have performed for the sake of another person. What did you lose that you could never get back? How does that compare to Christ's sacrifice?

1. Discuss the use of the word *agape* in the Bible.

   a. What does *agape* mean?

   b. What is the core idea of *agape*?

   c. What is the goal of *agape* love?

   d. Where is this word used in the Bible?

   e. Why is this important?

2. What are the eight reasons that love must be a top priority in our life? Discuss each reason.

   a. While this world is passing away, what will never pass away? (1 Corinthians 13:8)

   b. Examine what the Bible says about love in the following verses:

      • John 13:35

      • Galatians 5:6

- Ephesians 5:1-2

- Ephesians 5:25

3. Examine the church in Corinth and discuss the problem within that church.

    a. What did they have? (1 Corinthians 1:4-7)

    b. What did they lack? (1 Corinthians 13)

    c. What is love the bridge between? (1 Corinthians 12; 14)

    d. How can this relate to the Church and Christians today?

4. By what action did God demonstrate His love for this fallen world? (John 3:16)

    a. What is the greatest love one person can show another? (John 15:13)

    b. What obstacle did God overcome in loving us? (Romans 5:8)

c. Christ *died* for us "while we were still sinners." (Romans 5:8) How should this example convict us to live for Christ and love others that we might consider too sinful?

d. How did Christ show His love for human beings? (Galatians 2:20) What is the importance of the fact that "Christ lives in [us]"? Do we take this seriously? How?

e. Why should husbands live sacrificially toward their wives? (Ephesians 5:25)

5. In spite of how the world defines love, how do Christians know what love is? (1 John 3:16)

DID YOU KNOW?

In 1 Corinthians 13:1-3, Paul employs the figure of speech known as hyperbole: intentional exaggeration in order to make or illustrate a point. In verse 1 he suggests something that no one is capable of: speaking the languages of terrestrial beings (men) as well as the languages of celestial ones (angels). In verse 2, the word "all" is the key to his exaggeration: knowing "all mysteries and all knowledge" and having "all faith." And in verse 3, the same thing: giving "all my goods" to feed the poor. Even if we could do those things (and we can't), without love such acts and abilities would be meaningless.

THE PATIENCE AND KINDNESS OF LOVE

1 Corinthians 13:4-7

In this lesson we learn that true love is patient and kind.

OUTLINE

We live in a world where people are quick to retaliate when they are wronged and where kindnesses are done with an expectation of repayment. But God desires a different kind of love: love that is patient when wronged and love that extends kindness with no expectation of reward.

I. Love Is Longsuffering
   A. Examples of Longsuffering
   B. Encouragement to Be Longsuffering

II. Love Is Kind
   A. Examples of Kindness
   B. Encouragement to Be Kind

D r. Cecil Osborn has written a book entitled *The Art of Understanding Yourself*. In the book, he told about a couple who went to see a marriage counselor. With her husband sitting there listening to every word, the woman told the counselor, "I would like to have married a man who is very strong and yet very gentle. He would be strong enough to put me in my place when I get out of line, but understanding and sensitive enough to know when I need to have my own way in certain areas. He would be tolerant of my occasional outbursts and emotional tantrums, and wise enough to see that I need a good cry now and again. He would just pat me and console me without bothering to argue with me." She went on at considerable length, describing this paragon of virtue while her husband sat listening intently. When she finished listing all the traits she wished she had in her husband, the man said with a trace of bitterness, "There was someone like that once, but they crucified Him between two thieves." [1]

All of us would like to experience that level of perfection when it comes to love, especially in marriage and other close relationships. And it is toward that goal that the apostle Paul wrote 1 Corinthians 13 —the greatest treatise on love in the history of the world.

In verses 1-3 Paul pointed out how spiritual gifts and abilities without love are worthless. He revealed what the church at Corinth was but should not have been. In the next section, verses 4-7, Paul points out what the church was not yet should have been: a church characterized by love in action. In this lesson we will begin our journey through the characteristics of perfect love that Paul lists for the Corinthians.

What the husband said in the counseling room in the story above is accurate. If you read through verses 4-7 substituting the word "Christ" for the word "love," you will see that Paul is describing divine love. Only Christ can manifest perfect patience, kindness, and the rest of the qualities of pure love. And it is only when Christ lives in us that we can do the same (Galatians 2:20).

The primary thing to note as we go through verses 4-7 in this lesson and the lessons to come is that Paul is not defining love. Instead, he is displaying or demonstrating love. The fifteen qualities listed in verses 4-7 are examples of how love looks when it is practiced. This is not an academic discussion of definitions but an applicational discussion of desires—the desire to live a life that manifests the life of Jesus Christ who was love personified.

We begin with the first two qualities of love Paul lists in verse 4: "Love suffers long and is kind."

LOVE IS LONGSUFFERING

Not surprisingly, longsuffering (patience) is listed as one aspect of the fruit of the Spirit in Galatians 5:22. The Greek verb for "being patient" is *makrothumeo,* a combination of two words: long and passion. The combination of the words carries the idea of being under stress for a long period of time—thus the idea of suffering long or being patient. And Paul is saying that true love suffers long, is willing to endure, is patient—especially with people. *Makrothumeo* is most often used when referring to patience with people, not circumstances. And that is the kind of patience most of us need.

When dealing with people, we need the ability not to give way to anger and resentment; to suffer through those times without reacting negatively; to endure wrongs and injuries, nagging and criticism, irritations and unpleasantness. The Greeks of Paul's day were not familiar with this "suffering" kind of love. They considered a failure to respond to injury to be a weakness. Getting even and retaliating were expected. Aristotle, the Greek philosopher, taught that the great virtue was refusal to tolerate insult or injury and to strike back in retaliation at the slightest offense. Expectations are not much changed in modern cultures—strength is seen in defending one's turf, not in suffering long.

Examples of Longsuffering

God was patient with the human race in the days of Noah as Peter reminds us (1 Peter 3:20). God waited patiently for 120 years before sending the Great Flood upon the earth (Genesis 6:3). And Peter says God is doing the same today, being "longsuffering toward us, not willing that any should perish but that all should come to repentance" (2 Peter 3:9).

Many have wondered why God's hand of judgment has not moved against cultures such as our own where sin and immorality are displayed so flagrantly. There can be only one explanation: God is longsuffering.

A well-known nineteenth-century atheist named Robert Ingersoll used to include in his lectures this device: He would open his pocket watch and say, "I'll give God five minutes to strike me dead for the things I've said." When the five minutes were exhausted without judgment appearing, Ingersoll would use that as evidence that God doesn't exist. When the evangelist Theodore Parker heard of this, he said, "And did the gentleman think he could exhaust the patience of the eternal God in five minutes?" And he was right.[2]

New Testament examples of longsuffering are Stephen who, while being martyred, prayed that God would forgive his killers (Acts 7:60). Jesus, of course, is the other example from whom Stephen learned to forgive his persecutors (Luke 23:34).

Encouragement to Be Longsuffering

Both the Old and New Testaments provide ample encouragement for being patient—in the Old Testament, often noted by the phrase "slow to anger." Patient people have "great understanding" (Proverbs 14:29) and put "contention" to rest (Proverbs 15:18). The patient man's greatest virtue is to overlook a transgression (Proverbs 19:11), and the one who conquers his anger is better than the mighty who conquer a city (Proverbs 16:32).

In the New Testament we're told to "put on . . . longsuffering" (Colossians 3:12) and to exercise longsuffering toward "one another in love" (Ephesians 4:2). And Romans 12:17 says, "Repay no one evil for evil."

Here are some questions to help evaluate your current ability to be longsuffering:

- Do I demonstrate irritability or anger or have a quick temper?
- Does my love have a long fuse before the circuit blows? Do I know how to sit still and wait my turn? (Think about having to stand in line in stores.)
- Do I often give way to sarcasm when I have been hurt or when I am tired or when I am annoyed?
- Am I sometimes betrayed into speech and action that I later regret? (I'll admit to having written a few dozen letters in my life that I never mailed—and I'm glad I didn't.)
- Can I accept a fellow believer for who he is and realize that he, too, is moving in the direction of becoming Christlike?
- When I have been offended or my rights have been stepped on or I have been overlooked, do I find that I am thinking of ways to retaliate? (Even doing this mentally is a warning sign of trouble. The distance from a thought to an act is not far.)

Before Abraham Lincoln became President, he had a political opponent named Edwin Stanton who regularly slandered him in public. But when Lincoln became President, he chose Stanton to be his Secretary of War. When asked why, Lincoln said he chose Stanton because he was the best man for the job. Years later, when Lincoln was assassinated, Stanton said through his tears, "There lies the greatest ruler of men the world has ever seen." Lincoln was longsuffering with a man who hated him and won him over in the end.

LOVE IS KIND

The German philosopher Nietzsche hated Christianity for the way it encouraged people to be kind toward the weak. He wanted the weak to die out so that only the strong—the supermen—would remain. History saw in Adolf Hitler the expression of Nietzsche's philosophy. Jesus conquered men with the power of kindness and love, while Hitler destroyed them with the power of hate.

Kindness is one of the most powerful forces on earth. It can move a powerful person to humble himself and serve the weak and downtrodden with no expectation of repayment. It can move a person to wrap their arms around the poor and wretched of this world and bind their wounds. It can move a busy person to reach out to a lonely individual and become a friend. Kindness is active goodwill—reaching out even to one's enemies to extend pure love, restraining the desire to retaliate or seek vengeance.

There are many examples of kindness and encouragement to be kind throughout the Scriptures.

Examples of Kindness

Romans 2:4 says it is the "goodness" of God that leads us "to repentance." The very fact that nonbelievers repent of their sin and exercise faith in Jesus Christ is the result of the kindness of God. We don't deserve His kindness. We haven't done anything to earn it. In fact, our sin qualifies us for the opposite of God's kindness: His wrath. Yet God exercises His kindness to undeserving sinners nonetheless.

Titus 3:4-6 is a verse similar to John 3:16 in that it reveals the action by which God's emotion was demonstrated: "But when the kindness and the love of God our Savior toward man appeared." The kindness of God "appeared" in the Person of Jesus Christ who came to save us from our sins. God's love and kindness were demonstrated by the coming of Jesus. It's not enough to talk about kindness—it must be demonstrated. And 1 Peter 2:2-3 talks about tasting the grace (love, kindness) of God. When someone exercises kindness toward us, it is just as palpable as taking a cool drink on a hot day. We know someone has done something special for us.

God is the greatest example of a kind "person" we could ever hope to see. From Him we learn what it means to exercise kindness toward the least deserving of all.

Encouragement to Be Kind

Luke 6:27-36 contains some of Jesus' most profound words on kindness along with several examples of how to be kind. This is the passage that contains such well-known exhortations as "love your enemies . . . bless those who curse you . . . . offer the other [cheek] . . . . do not withhold your tunic . . . . give to everyone who asks of you . . . . as you want men to do to you, you also do to them likewise . . . . do good, and lend, hoping for nothing in return . . . . be merciful, just as your Father also is merciful."

This passage reminds us that there ought to be a difference in how Christians treat people, and not just people of the faith—but all people. If we are kind only to those who are kind toward us, we have missed the point of Jesus' teaching. The world will lend and be kind to those who can repay. Jesus says we should do more— lend and be kind to those who cannot repay. When we are kind to those who are unkind to us (our enemies), we are doing something totally different from what the world would do.

But we are also to be kind to those within the faith family, as Paul wrote to the Ephesians: "And be kind to one another, tenderhearted, forgiving one another, even as God in Christ forgave you" (4:32). J. R. Miller has written these words which are apropos to the subject of kindness: "Do not keep the alabaster boxes of your affection sealed and laid away until your friends are dead. Fill their days with tenderness. Speak words of commendation while their ears can hear them. If my friends have any vases laid away filled with the perfumes of sympathy and affection which they intend to break over my dead body, I would far rather they would bring them out along my toilsome days and open them when I can enjoy them and be refreshed by them." [3]

Consider these practical questions as you assess your own "kindness quotient":

- Do I offer to help before I am asked?
- Am I thoughtful and considerate?

- Do I call when I will be late or before I unexpectedly change the family's dinner plans? (Men should pay special attention to this one.)
- Am I concerned with doing little things for people?
- Do I have a pleasant tone in my voice? Do I lash out or rip another person apart with harsh, critical language? Am I sarcastic?
- Do I express my appreciation for my extended family members, friends, and coworkers with verbal and non-verbal expressions of thanks and kindness?

Patience and kindness—two qualities of life that God imparts to those who love as He loves.

Notes

1. Cecil G. Osborne, *The Art of Understanding Yourself* (Grand Rapids: Zondervan Publishing House, 1967), 146.

2. John MacArthur, audiocassette "Perfect Love—The Qualities of True Love, Part 1," n.d.

3. J. R. Miller, *Week-Day Religion* (Oliphant, Anderson, & Ferrier, 1887), 4. http://week-day-religion.jr-miller.com/16-kindness-that-comes-too-late-4.html.

1. Do you think you have the ability to be longsuffering? How can you become a more patient person? Is patience something you can work on?

   a. What does Paul say the church at Corinth should have been characterized by in 1 Corinthians 13:4-7?

   b. In what type of situation do you struggle to be patient? What is a plausible way you can work on being more patient when confronted with that type of situation?

   c. Write down a list of questions you should ask yourself before responding negatively in any given situation. (Is my current attitude God-honoring? What is the root of my anger? How can I respond in a way that displays Christlike patience?) How can you train yourself to remember these questions when you are angered? How can this help you respond with divine love?

2. Read Matthew 18:21-35.

   a. What virtue in the king did the debtor call upon when threatened with judgment? (verse 26)

   b. How did the king exercise the patience he was asked to demonstrate? (verse 27)

c. Had the debtor asked that the debt be forgiven? In what ways are patience and forgiveness synonyms?

d. When the debtor was freed by the king, what did he go out and demand of one who owed him a small debt? (verse 28)

e. What virtue was the freed debtor asked to demonstrate by the one who owed him money? (verse 29)

f. What was the freed debtor's response? (verse 30)

g. How is this parable an illustration of Paul's words in Ephesians 4:32? Whom does the king represent in this parable? (verse 35) The freed debtor? The debtor's friend?

h. In what ways can you compare yourself to the debtor? Do you demonstrate God's patience toward others?

i. What practical application do you find in the interplay between patience and forgiveness in this parable? When you are patient with another person, in what way are you forgiving that person?

1. Discuss the different ways patience is encouraged in the following verses:

   • Proverbs 14:29

   • Proverbs 15:18

   • Proverbs 19:11

   • Proverbs 16:32

2. Discuss the meaning of being "like-minded" in Romans 15:5. That is, what attitude does God want us to have toward one another?

3. What does Paul say the church at Corinth should have been characterized by in 1 Corinthians 13:4-7?

   a. Are these qualities evident in our churches today?

   b. What does being "the elect of God" have to do with our responsibility to be kind? (Colossians 3:12)

c. Should there be a difference in the way Christians treat others as opposed to non-Christians? Is there a difference?

d. How patient was God with humanity in the days of Noah? (Genesis 6:3) How patient has He been with us?

e. The Greek verb *makrothnumeo* ("being patient") is a combination of which two words? What can we learn about patience from this definition?

f. How has Christianity's view on patience differed from those of other cultures in history? Is this applicable to our world today in any way?

4. Read and discuss the following Scriptures. What does each reveal about what it means to exercise longsuffering toward one another?

- Colossians 3:12

- Ephesians 4:2

- Ephesians 4:32

- Romans 12:17

5. What attribute of God leads us to repentance? (Romans 2:4) By which action did God demonstrate His kindness toward us?

   a. Are we deserving of God's kindness? (Titus 3:4-6) What does this tell us about the love of God?

   b. What specific examples of kindness does Jesus provide in Luke 6:27-36? Discuss ways that you could demonstrate Christ's kindness in your workplace, neighborhood, or community.

DID YOU KNOW?

The Greek word Paul uses for kindness in 1 Corinthians 13:4 is a rare word: *chresteuomai*. This is the only place where it occurs in the New Testament. The literal meaning of the word is to show oneself to be mild (of temperament), and, therefore, kind. This verb is derived from the adjective *chrestos* which meant literally "fit for use" or "virtuous, good." Figuratively, it meant to be manageable, that is, mild or pleasant. When Jesus commented on the difference between old wine and new wine, He said, "The old is better *[chrestos]*" (Luke 5:39). A kind person is one who gets better with age.

LOVE'S POWER OVER ENVY

1 Corinthians 13:4

In this lesson we learn the dangers of envy and jealousy and how to replace them with agape *love.*

OUTLINE

The temptation to want what we don't have is as old as the Garden of Eden. Adam and Eve wanted God's knowledge and the tree's fruit—and envied the serpent's freedom to have it all. Envy and jealousy are two sins that can ultimately destroy the one who embraces them.

I. Jealousy Travels in Circles
   A. Jealousy Travels in Possessions Circles
   B. Jealousy Travels in Power Circles
   C. Jealousy Travels in Performing Circles
   D. Jealousy Travels in Professional Circles
   E. Jealousy Travels in Paternal Circles

II. Jealousy Destroys Love

III. Jealousy Can Be Replaced
   A. Renounce Jealousy as Sin
   B. Release Your Loved Ones Who Are Caught in the Jaws of Your Jealousy
   C. Remember Your Rival in Prayer Every Day
   D. Reaffirm God's Goodness to You, and Learn to Be Content
   E. Rekindle God's Love in Your Heart Through Prayer and Reading of God's Word

There is a Latin proverb that says envy is the enemy of honor. William Shakespeare called envy the green sickness. Philip Bailey, the eloquent English poet of another time, vividly described jealousy as a coal that comes "hissing hot from hell." Someone else has written that envy is the uneasiness of the mind caused by the consideration of a goodly desire, but which somebody else obtains. We get envious, or jealous, when someone else obtains that which we have desired for ourselves.

In his discussion of love in 1 Corinthians 13, Paul has already given us two positive characteristics of love: Love is patient and love is kind (verse 4). He now turns from the positive to the negative, looking at eight feelings or actions that will never be found in *agape* love. These are enemies of *agape,* and the first one is envy. *Agape* love—true, godly, sacrificial love—will never be envious of another.

The Greek verb for being envious *(zeloo)* comes from the Greek root word *zeo,* a word that means "to boil, seethe, or be hot." Connected to the same root is *zelos,* which means "zeal or jealously." The context determines whether *zeo* is a positive or negative emotion. Positively, it could be enthusiasm or a good kind of zeal. Negatively, it always refers to a seething, boiling jealousy or envy. The emotion is neutral—we make it positive or negative by the motivation behind it and the manner in which it's expressed. The difference between *zealous* and *jealous* is just one letter—but they are worlds apart in results.

The subject of envy and jealousy in Paul's discussion of love came from what he had learned about the church at Corinth. There were all kinds of divisions in the church—and the root of divisions is often jealousy and envy. So Paul is pointing out to them that envy and jealousy have no place among those who claim to love with God's kind of love.

To be more accurate, while envy and jealousy are often used interchangeably, there are some differences in how we can look at them:

- Envy is at the bottom wishing it was at the top; jealousy is at the top resenting anyone who might try to replace it.

- Envy is angry at what everyone else has that it doesn't have; jealousy is afraid that what it has will be taken away.

- Envy mourns its empty hands and rejoices when others lose what they have; jealousy rejoices at its full hands but is fearful of losing it all to someone else.

Both envy and jealousy are incapable of rejoicing over another's success. Scripture tells us we are to weep with those who weep and rejoice with those who rejoice (Romans 12:15; 1 Corinthians 12:26). But jealousy and envy reverse that sympathetic notion: They weep with those who rejoice and rejoice with those who weep!

In this lesson we'll dissect the negative emotion of jealousy and learn how to replace it with something better.

JEALOUSY TRAVELS IN CIRCLES

When we say someone travels in the "circle of" a certain kind of person, we know what that means—people who can often be found together. Well, jealousy has a circle in which it travels, and that circle is made up of possessions, power, performance, professionalism, and paternal figures.

Jealousy Travels in Possessions Circles

In Genesis 26:14 we read, "For [Isaac] had possessions of flocks and possessions of herds and a great number of servants. So the Philistines envied him." The Philistines were no paupers themselves, yet when they saw what Isaac had, they were envious. Envious people never have enough. When they see someone who has more than they have, they cannot rest for wishing they had it for themselves.

Jealousy Travels in Power Circles

After the Israelites came out of Egypt with Moses as their leader, there were those who "envied Moses in the camp" (Psalm 106:16). Korah and a group of "two hundred and fifty leaders of the congregation" (Numbers 16:2) rose up against Moses because they envied his position of leadership. Throughout the Old Testament history of Israel's and Judah's kings, you find those seeking the place of the king out of envy. Envy makes people do terrible things, things they wouldn't have dreamt of doing under other circumstances.

In the New Testament we find religious leaders persecuting Jesus and the leaders of the Early Church out of jealousy: "The high priest and his officials, who were Sadducees, were filled with jealousy" (Acts 5:17, NLT). When people have power and popularity that we don't have, there is a temptation and tendency to be envious. We see power struggles everywhere, even in the contemporary church.

Jealousy Travels in Performing Circles

When Rachel, one of Jacob's wives, heard that her sister Leah, also married to Jacob, had given birth to sons while Rachel was still barren, "Rachel envied her sister" (Genesis 30:1). And King Saul spent years trying to kill David, a young man he once loved, because he was so jealous of David's growing popularity in Israel (1 Samuel 18:7-8). David killed Goliath, who had been tormenting Israel, when Saul had been unable to do anything about the giant. The people rejoiced, but Saul eventually was enraged.

I read in *Reader's Digest* about a mother of four who was talking about her neighbor who had four children. She said, "She is amazing. Her house is always neat as a pin. She is a wonderful cook. She does her own sewing. Her children are polite and well-behaved. She is active in the PTA, helps with the Brownies, and is a den mother for the Cub Scouts. She is pretty and has loads of personality. She makes me sick!" That's a good example of jealousy rooted in performance.

Jealousy Travels in Professional Circles

When Paul was in prison in Rome, certain unscrupulous preachers took advantage of the situation and began to try to usurp his leadership position. Paul noted that "some indeed preach Christ even from envy and strife" (Philippians 1:15). These preachers were envious of Paul's stature in the church, and they sought to capitalize on his imprisonment by gathering audiences for themselves. For Paul's part, he was just thankful the Gospel was being preached, regardless of motive (verse 18).

A great American preacher of an earlier day, T. DeWitt Talmadge, wrote about the fate of another eminent preacher and Bible commentator, Dr. Albert Barnes, a godly Presbyterian pastor in Philadelphia from 1830–1867. Barnes' denomination put him on trial on the basis of an alleged doctrinal issue and sentenced him not to preach in his church for a year. He had to sit in the pew and listen to others speak from his pulpit. But Talmadge described the real reason behind Barnes' trial: professional jealousy. Talmadge wrote, "The pretended offense that he did not believe in a limited atonement was not the real offense. The real offense was this: It was that all the men who tried him put together could not possibly equal Albert Barnes."

Jealousy, if allowed, will flourish in professional circles.

Jealousy Travels in Paternal Circles

I have found more instances of jealousy in paternal (family) settings than in any other context in the Bible. We begin with Cain's jealousy of Abel, resulting in Abel's murder (Genesis 4), followed by Ishmael's mocking of Isaac (Genesis 21)—a jealous feud that persists to this day between Arabs and Jews. At birth Jacob seized the heel of his twin, Esau, typifying his later aspirations for Esau's superior birthright (Genesis 25). Jesus' own brothers rejected Him because of whom He claimed to be (Mark 3:21). In the parable of the prodigal son, the elder brother is dripping with jealousy over the father's treatment of the younger brother: "Lo, these many years I have been serving you . . . and yet you never gave me a young goat, that I might make merry with my friends" (Luke 15:29).

Perhaps the greatest illustration is the story of Joseph, the favorite son of his father Jacob. Joseph's brothers were so jealous of Joseph's favored position and the dreams Joseph had concerning his future superiority that they feigned his death and sold him into slavery (Acts 7:9). It was a horrible act motivated by jealousy.

Be careful! Jealously travels in circles. There are some people of whom you will never be jealous, but those in your circles are good candidates. Practice rejoicing in their blessings and favor—and praying for them. It's impossible to remain jealous of someone for whom you are praying.

JEALOUSY DESTROYS LOVE

Jealousy gets its foot in the door by destroying love. No one would ever follow through on a jealous impulse if they had not first abandoned love in their heart. Cain, Abel, Ishmael, Jacob, Joseph's brothers, Korah, Jewish religious leaders, and on and on. No one committed to loving God and loving his neighbor will yield to the temptation to be envious or jealous. Jealousy is a cruel monster that will destroy love if allowed.

Jealousy can certainly hurt the person toward whom it is directed, but the greatest harm is done to the jealous person himself. Like any negative emotion that is allowed to flourish in the absence of love, jealousy will eventually destroy the one who embraces it. King Saul of Israel is a prime example: His jealousy of David grew so intense that he found himself mentally and psychologically disturbed, resorting to attempted murder to remove the object of his jealousy.

Jealousy destroys love—and the one who yields to its all-consuming carnal lusts. But the good news is that jealousy can be replaced in the heart where it has taken hold.

JEALOUSY CAN BE REPLACED

There are five practices that will remove jealousy from the human heart so that *agape* love can reign.

Renounce Jealousy as Sin

Jealousy is not a personality disorder or something you inherited from your parents. Jealousy is sin. Matthew 27:18 says that Pontius Pilate knew the Jewish leaders handed Jesus over to be crucified because of envy. There couldn't be a clearer example of the carnality and sinfulness of envy. If you want a specific commandment that envy and jealousy violate, try the fourth commandment of the ten given through Moses: "You shall not covet . . . anything that is your neighbor's" (Exodus 20:17). Coveting is a sin against God because it shows a lack of gratitude for what God has provided.

Release Your Loved Ones Who Are Caught in the Jaws of Your Jealousy

I have seen jealousy develop in marriages when the wife begins to develop her own talents and abilities, sometimes overshadowing those of her husband; and the husband's jealousy tries to force her back down into a "safe" posture, one that is not threatening to him. Ann Morrow was married to the famous pioneering pilot Charles Lindberg. For many years, he was the famous one in their marriage. But then she became widely known and honored as an author. And she credited the love and support of Charles Lindberg for supporting the development of her gifts. Jealousy binds, but love liberates.

Remember Your Rival in Prayer Every Day

A famous preacher named F. B. Meyer was envious of the skills and success of another famous preacher, G. Campbell Morgan. Meyer wrote later that he only overcame his envy by praying for his rival like this: "Oh, God, bless that man so much that I can flourish from the overflow of his crowds into my church." When you can pray for your rival's success, you are on the way to defeating jealousy.

Reaffirm God's Goodness to You, and Learn to Be Content

One word is the antithesis of envy and jealousy: contentment. Content people do not envy or become jealous of others. The next time envy or jealousy begin creeping into your heart, displacing *agape* love, do an inventory—look for the discontent that is fueling your covetousness. We only want what others have when we have lost sight of what God has provided for us. Thanksgiving is the antidote to envy and jealousy.

Rekindle God's Love in Your Heart Through Prayer and Reading of God's Word

The divorce rate in America is evidence of a complete misunderstanding of the nature of true love. People decide to leave their marriage because they don't "feel" in love the way they used to. Or they think they've fallen out of love. When that happens, it usually means that they didn't understand love when they got married—that they married on the basis of *phileo* (affection or feeling) and not *agape* (the commitment of the will to seek another person's best interests).

Agape love can be learned and cultivated. And when the legitimate feelings of love that accompany true commitment begin to wane due to inattention, disappointment, or conflict, *agape* can be rekindled. How? Through prayer and the study of God's Word.

If the flower of *agape* is to grow and blossom in your heart, then the weeds of envy and jealousy must be pulled up immediately.

1. What are the eight "enemies" of *agape* that Paul lists in 1 Corinthians 13? Have you ever found yourself caught up in any of these?

   a. According to the lesson, what is the difference between envy and jealousy?

   b. Do you have a problem with either? What have you been envious or jealous about?

   c. If you're not careful, how can envy or jealousy consume you? What are the dangers? Are you ever satisfied or happy when you are envious or jealous?

   d. What are envy and jealousy incapable of doing that we are told to do in Romans 12:15? What do envy and jealousy do instead?

   e. What does the Bible say about feelings of jealousy? (Exodus 20:17)

   f. What does the example in Matthew 27:16-18 reveal about envy?

g. What are five practices, according to the lesson, that can help remove jealousy from your heart?

h. List all the people you may currently be jealous/envious of. Write down all the things you admire about them, and then pray over each person. Pray for their success and (genuinely) thank God for them. Try to pray for them as often as you can.

i. Make a list of all the things you have that others might not. (These don't have to be material things; they can be things like family, friends, food, etc.) Thank God for all of these blessings He has given you. Make this prayer a constant habit.

2. What role does choice play in understanding the source of envy? (Proverbs 3:31) Why is understanding this important?

a. How can envy impact one's health? Conversely, what does a "sound heart" offer? (Proverbs 14:30)

b. What wordplay do you find between *zealous* and *jealous* in Proverbs 23:17?

c. How does the destructive power of jealousy compare with wrath and anger? (Proverbs 27:4)

GROUP QUESTIONS

1. According to the lesson, in what circles does jealousy travel? Discuss and list examples of each from the Bible and in today's time.

   -

   -

   -

   -

   -

2. Read Psalm 73:1-28.

   a. What almost caused the psalmist to lose his spiritual bearings? (verse 3)

   b. List and discuss some of the things he envied when he looked at the lives of the godless around him.

      - verses 4-5: In the material and physical realm...

      - verse 12: In their lifestyle...

c. How serious were the effects of his envy? (verses 14, 21-22)

d. What success did he have in understanding why the wicked seemed to prosper? (verse 16) Do you ever struggle with understanding why the wicked seem to prosper?

e. When did he begin to gain insight and God's perspective? (verse 17)

f. What did he come to understand about those he had envied? (verses 18-20, 27) Discuss how this can help us understand things in life that might seem unfair to us.

g. What did he begin to grasp as his source of assurance and contentment? (verses 23-24)

h. Instead of desiring what others had, what did he discover was his one true desire? (verse 25)

i. Why is God worthy of being all we desire? (verse 26) Discuss why understanding this verse is important.

3. What kind of lifestyle is it easy to become envious of at times?

    a. What do those lifestyles offer?

    b. Why is that appealing?

4. Translate Psalm 73:17 into your own words as a way to deal with envy. Share with the rest of the group.

DID YOU KNOW?

Many Bible readers are surprised when they find God referred to as a "jealous God" (Exodus 20:5; 34:14; Deuteronomy 4:24; 5:9; 6:15; Joshua 24:19). We are (correctly) used to thinking of jealousy in negative terms because of how sinful humans use jealousy—which is what sets God's jealousy apart from ours. Our jealousy is self-centered; we are usually jealous because of our insecurity and greed. When God is jealous, it is not for His benefit, but ours. He does not want us worshiping idols because He knows their corrupting influence. In the same way parents are "jealous" for their teenager's moral purity, so God is jealous for ours.

LOVE'S POWER
OVER PRIDE

1 Corinthians 13:4

In this lesson we learn why pride is the enemy of love.

OUTLINE

There's a thin line between striving for excellence in life—and pride. We should try to maximize the gifts and abilities God has given us, but when our striving becomes self-serving, we have crossed the line. Pride can destroy *agape* love and give God a reason to remove His blessing.

  I. **Pride Ignores God's Sovereignty**

 II. **Pride Invites God's Judgment**

III. **Pride Interrupts God's Peace and Love**

 IV. **Application**

Paul continues detailing the weeds that will grow up in the garden of the heart, choking out *agape* love—and the next is pride: "Love does not parade itself, is not puffed up" (verse 4). Parading oneself before others is the external manifestation of pride; being "puffed up" is one's own internal estimation of self-importance.

C. S. Lewis wrote these words about the vice of pride:

> There is one vice of which no man in the world is free, which everyone in the world simply loathes when he sees it in someone else, and of which hardly any people except Christians ever imagine that they are guilty themselves. I have heard people admit that they are bad tempered, or that they can't keep their heads about girls, or drink, or even that they are cowards. I don't think I have ever heard anyone who is not a Christian accuse himself of the vice of pride, and, at the same time, I have very seldom met someone who was not a Christian who showed the slightest mercy to it in others. There is no fault which makes a man more unpopular, and no fault which we are more unconscious of in ourselves, and the more we have it ourselves, the more we dislike it in others.[1]

Pride may be the sin that shows up most consistently throughout the Bible. At the top of the list of the "six things the Lord hates" in Proverbs is "a proud look" (Proverbs 6:16-17). Jesus said that pride is one of the things that emanates from the heart of man, defiling him in the process (Mark 7:22).

Someone in my church once gave me a definition of pride that casts a unique light on this self-centered sin: "Pride is avoiding necessary character changes by expecting others to fit their ideas and feelings around mine." Pride is consumed with making the world revolve around one's self. As a result, pride has no time to consider the needs of others—the basic characteristic of *agape* love. Therefore, pride becomes the enemy of true love.

Paul uses an unusual phrase—"puffed up"—to describe this vaunted, internal perspective that characterizes pride. He used it previously in 1 Corinthians 5:2 where he addressed the immorality that was present in the church at Corinth. Too often the emphasis in 1 Corinthians 5 is misread. It is not the sin of the individual accused of immorality that was Paul's main focus, but it was the way the church at large tolerated the sin and didn't excise it. Yes, the person's immorality was sin—but Paul wanted to correct whatever thinking had allowed the sin to persist in the church.

Paul reproved the Corinthians for being so "puffed up" (1 Corinthians 5:2)—so pridefully sophisticated—that they felt no shame or grief over what was happening. They were acting like sexual immorality was just part of the culture—part of the "way things are in this world." That's right! But it's not the way things are to be in the church. The Corinthians' pride got in the way of their spiritual understanding.

In 1 Corinthians 8:1 Paul says, "Knowledge puffs up, but love edifies." *Edify*, of course, means to "build up." So Paul says you can choose to be puffed up or you can build up others. The Corinthians were elevating their supposed knowledge and intellects above their love for one another. But knowledge without love leads to pride. (See 1 Corinthians 13:2; Colossians 2:18.) This is a powerful warning for those in our modern age who value intellectual prowess above all.

The Greek word behind "puffed up" is *phusioo* that suggests the image of a blacksmith's bellows filled with air to stoke the flames of a fire. Or in our day it might bring to mind a giant balloon filled with air to the point of bursting. The word literally means to blow up or inflate. In the personal, spiritual sense, it suggests a person who walks around with his chest stuck out, inflated with the idea of his own superiority to others. Nothing is so unpleasant to be around as a puffed-up person. We want nothing more than to stick a pin in him and deflate him, allowing the air of self-importance to escape.

There are three truths taught in Scripture about the danger of pride: what it ignores, what it invites, and what it interrupts.

Pride Ignores God's Sovereignty

When we act pridefully, we act as if we had something to do with what we have or what we know, as if we could take credit in some way for who we are. And to think like that is to ignore God's sovereignty as the ruler over all. Paul took up this issue with the Corinthians when he asked them some pointed questions in 1 Corinthians 4:7.

- Question 1: "For who makes you differ from one another?"

  That is, what makes you think you are superior to others? God is the source of each person's unique individuality. It is

He who has blessed each of us with our unique gifts and abilities, making each person special in his or her own way. When we start taking an arrogant sort of pride in who we are, we take credit as if we had something to do with our own uniqueness.

- Question 2: "And what do you have that you did not receive?"

That is, what do you have that didn't come from God? Where did your ability, your beauty, your intelligence, and your wealth come from? King David said that everything we have comes from God (1 Chronicles 29:10-16). John the Baptist said, "A man can receive nothing unless it has been given to him from heaven" (John 3:27). James wrote, "Every good gift and every perfect gift is from above, and comes down from the Father of lights" (James 1:17). To believe that we are responsible for who we are is the height of pride.

- Question 3: "Now if you did indeed receive it, why do you boast as if you had not received it?"

That is, if you received who you are as a gift from God, why do you puff yourself up as if you had something to do with your own health or wealth? By the world's standards, the Corinthians might have had reasons to boast, but Christians don't live by the world's standards. If we are going to live by the *agape* standard, we have to begin with a humble and grateful spirit toward a generous God from whom all our blessings flow. Proud people cannot love sacrificially. There is not room in the human heart for serving pride and *agape* at the same time (Matthew 6:24).

PRIDE INVITES GOD'S JUDGMENT

Pride is a sin that seems to be an open invitation for God's intervention in judgment. The book of Proverbs, especially, warns against the downfall of the proud (3:34; 8:13; 11:2; 16:5, 18; 29:23). It's not surprising that we find all these proverbs summarized in the most "Jewish" of the New Testament epistles, the letter of James: "But He gives more grace. Therefore He says: 'God resists the proud, but gives grace to the humble' " (4:6, quoting Proverbs 3:34).

If you want to know what you can do to have God resist your every move, James 4:6 tells you: Be a prideful, arrogant person. I have seen more instances than I care to remember of individuals in Christian ministry who had a hard time finding the humility switch in their life. And looking back, I can see how God resisted their efforts to promote themselves and their ministries and how they faded into obscurity. We all are tempted with pride, and we all have to self-correct and humble ourselves on occasion. But if we fail to do that over time and insist on being "puffed up," God will step in and judge the pride.

The story of King Nebuchadnezzar of Babylon (Daniel 4) is one of the best examples in Scripture of how God deals with pride. Nebuchadnezzar was ruler of the greatest kingdom in the world, with Babylon as its capital. The city was 15 miles square with walls nearly 400 feet high and 85 feet across. Chariots, four abreast, could be driven around the top of the city walls! The Euphrates River entered the city on one side and exited on the other, providing plenty of water for the million-plus residents. Historians say Babylon's farms were so productive that they had a twenty-year supply of food in storage. Nebuchadnezzar's air-conditioned "hanging gardens," a gift for his wife, were one of the wonders of the ancient world.

And the king was boastfully proud of it all: "Is not this great Babylon, that I have built for a royal dwelling by my mighty power and for the honor of my majesty?" (Daniel 4:30) If you'll read the rest of the story, you'll find that it wasn't long before Nebuchadnezzar had been reduced to insanity, crawling around eating grass like a beast of the field. God had had enough of his pride and arrogance. Nebuchadnezzar eventually repented of his self-glorification, but it took the humbling hand of God to make it happen.

Pride appears to have been the "original sin" in the universe. When Lucifer (Satan) was a member of God's heavenly court, he rose up against God and five times declared his intent to exalt himself above God: "I will . . . I will . . . I will . . . I will . . . I will" (Isaiah 14:12-14). The next thing we know, Lucifer has been cast out of heaven to earth. Pride will not be sanctioned in heaven.

A similar thing happened to Herod in the New Testament. After delivering an oration from his throne, the people began shouting, "The voice of a god and not of a man!" (Acts 12:22) And "because he did not give glory to God. . . . He was eaten by worms and died" (verse 23). Herod willingly accepted praise that belonged to God alone and was judged for it.

C. S. Lewis wrote these words about putting one's self in opposition to God: "You come up against something which is in every respect immeasurably superior to yourself. Unless you know God as that—and, therefore, know yourself as nothing in comparison—you do not know God at all. As long as you are proud, you cannot know God. A proud man is always looking down on things and down on people; and, of course, as long as you are looking down, you cannot see something that is above you." [2]

Every Christian, when going through times of difficulty and testing, should ask himself whether he is experiencing God's hand against pride. Because pride is what God seems to judge most quickly, it is always worth checking.

Pride Interrupts God's Peace and Love

By its very nature, pride is competitive. Pride thinks it is the greatest one in the room or church or company or community. And when someone else appears who might appear qualified to take that position away, pride kicks into gear. This is what sets pride apart from other vices—it is the only one that is competitive at heart. People aren't proud of being rich—they're proud of being richer than everyone else. Pride thrives on comparison and remaining on top.

Think about a guy and a girl who are dating. The guy decides the relationship just isn't working out, so he has a speech prepared with which he's going to break off the relationship. But before he can get around to doing that, another guy asks the girl out and she says "Yes." Now he's ready to fight like crazy to keep the girl. Why? Because his pride has been wounded! The fact that his girlfriend would dare go out with another guy means she must be thinking the same thing he's thinking—that their relationship isn't going to work out. A few days earlier that would have been great— it would have made his breaking up with her that much easier. But now, he's totally changed. He wants her back, but not because he loves her. Because his pride has been attacked. He's got to prove that he's better than this other guy who just entered the picture. Pride makes people do unbelievable things!

If you want to lose your peace, spend the rest of your life trying to be better than everyone else. If you want to keep your peace and experience God's blessing, live a humble life, content with who God created you to be.

Application

Pride and *agape* love cannot coexist in the same heart. Neither can pride and humility. And pride is a cue for God to withdraw His blessing. Choose today to humble yourself before God and others. That is the cue for God's grace to be poured out upon you and for the *agape* love of God to fill your heart.

Notes

1. Subsequently published: C. S. Lewis, *Readings for Meditation and Reflection* (San Francisco: Harper San Francisco, 1996), 79.

2. C. S. Lewis, *Mere Christianity* (San Francisco: Harper Collins, 2001), 124.

PERSONAL QUESTIONS

1. What is the second "weed" that Paul warned about in
   1 Corinthians 13:4?

   a. What is the definition of being "puffed up"? What does the
      lesson tell us about the amount of times this sin shows up
      throughout the Bible? Why do you think this is?

   b. What is at the top of the list of the "six things the Lord hates"?
      (Proverbs 6:16-17)

   c. What does the Bible say about pride in Mark 7:22-23?

   d. What are you most likely to feel prideful about in your life—
      family, accomplishments, position? Who should get the credit?

   e. Is your pride tied to anything else in your life (insecurity,
      selfishness, etc.)? How can you let go of pride? What actions
      can you take?

2. Read 1 Chronicles 29:10-20.

   a. What had David done that led up to this prayer?
      (1 Chronicles 29:2-5)

b. Since David was richer than anyone as king, how might he have been tempted to feel about his actions—prideful or humble?

c. What did the leaders and people of Israel do when they saw what David did? (1 Chronicles 29:6-8)

d. How did the people and the king respond to their actions? (1 Chronicles 29:9)

e. If you struggle with pride, how can you learn from David's prayer in 1 Chronicles 29:10-20?

f. List the number of instances in which David makes reference to God being the source of all things in this prayer. Would making a list of things God is responsible for in your life help you give Him due credit?

g. Why is it impossible to be prideful about what you do/give/accomplish while repeating David's words in verses 11-13?

h. Why does the human heart incline toward self-elevation? (Jeremiah 17:9)

1. Discuss the different ways this lesson describes pride.

    a. What did C. S. Lewis say about pride?

    b. How is being prideful also selfish?

    c. What picture does the Greek word *phusioo* paint about pride?

    d. How can pride become a segue into other sins?

2. What does Paul reprimand the church at Corinth for in 1 Corinthians 5:2?

    a. What does Paul say about pride in 1 Corinthians 8:1? What does knowledge without love lead to? Consider the contrast between pride and love.

    b. What does pride ignore? Discuss the three questions Paul asks in 1 Corinthians 4:7. Why is it important to acknowledge God as the One from whom all our blessings flow?

c. What does pride invite? Discuss the examples found in this lesson. Who was boastful and what happened to him? What was the "original sin" in the universe?

d. What does pride interrupt? Review the danger that could lead to. What sort of heart does pride promote? What does pride thrive on? What is the only way we can experience peace?

e. For those who want God's blessing, what is the first requirement in the list in 2 Chronicles 7:14?

3. Read Isaiah 14:12-15.

a. List and discuss the five things Lucifer purposed to do in the presence of God (verses 13-14).

- I will

- I will

- I will

- I will

- I will

b. Which direction did he end up traveling that was the opposite of his desire? (verse 15) What can happen to us if we let our pride consume us? Will we end up in the place we most desire?

4. What will be Lucifer's ultimate destination? (Revelation 20:10)

5. How is his experience an illustration (and warning) of James 4:6?

DID YOU KNOW?

The Hebrew root verb for being proud is *g'h*—from it come the noun and adjective referring to those who are proud. The verb literally means to rise up (like the sea or a river) or to grow up (like a plant). In Job 40:12 the Lord used a play on words when he said to Job, "Look on everyone who is proud [lifted up], and bring him low." The Hebrew root for humble is *anv* from which come the verb, noun, and adjective. It means poor, afflicted, or lowly. Twice Lucifer said, "I will ascend" (Isaiah 14:13-14), but Jesus saw him "fall like lightning from heaven" (Luke 10:18). Those who lift themselves up will find themselves cast down.

LOVE'S POWER OVER RUDENESS

1 Corinthians 13:5

*In this lesson we learn why courtesy
is an important part of love.*

OUTLINE

We often read of the "dumbing down" of cultures from an academic
or intellectual perspective. But courtesy can be dumbed down as
well. That happens when we mistake courtesy as a synonym for
manners that change constantly. The truth is, courtesy is a synonym
for love.

   I. **Courtesy Is Love's Symmetry**

  II. **Courtesy Is Love's Simplicity**

 III. **Courtesy Is Love's Sensitivity**

 IV. **Application**

Years ago an author named Marabel Morgan wrote *The Total Woman*—a book that caused no small amount of discussion. The theme of the book was what wives could do to inject new energy into their marriage. And some of her ideas were a bit unconventional, to say the least. Another book she wrote was titled *The Electric Woman*, again on the subject of women and their marriages.

One of the chapters in *The Electric Woman* is titled "The Evolution of Marriage" in which the author shows the devolution of common courtesies between husbands and wives the longer they are married. She created a chart to show how different aspects of marriage change from the honeymoon to one year later and then ten years later:

- Meals: honeymoon, a romantic restaurant; one year later, fast food; ten years later, frozen dinners.

- Romantic times: honeymoon, late-night pizza; one year later, late-night feedings; ten years later, late-night fights.

- Travel: honeymoon, an exotic trip; one year later, trip to the mall; ten years later, reading *National Geographic.*

- Passion: honeymoon, sizzle; one year later, piddle; ten years later, fizzle.

- Communication: honeymoon, sweet, soft nothings; one year later, sweet nothings; ten years later, nothings.

- Sex: honeymoon, passion; one year later, apathy; ten years later, atrophy.[1]

Do you get the drift? Marabel Morgan is saying that, if we're not careful, the kind and loving things we do in the early stages of a relationship when we are "in love" can deteriorate. Indeed, sometimes we are more courteous and kind to a stranger than we are to those to whom we have committed ourselves to love. Somehow we stop choosing to put the other person first, stop choosing to live sacrificially, stop choosing to love with *agape* love.

We saw in the beginning of these lessons that love is the priority: "The greatest of these is love" (1 Corinthians 13:13). Great things accomplished without *agape* love are worthless, Paul wrote (verses 1-3). And now we are in the process of learning what true love really is. Paul started off by listing two things that love is (patient and kind), and then took the opposite tack by talking about what love is not. We've seen that love doesn't envy, is not prideful. And in this lesson we will see that love "does not behave rudely" (verse 5).

The King James Version says that love "doth not behave itself unseemly." And we say "Amen!" without really knowing what those words mean. The Greek for "unseemly" is tied to our English words *scheme* or *schematic*, referring to the shape of something. While newer translations render Paul's words as "love is not rude," his words literally mean "love is not without shape."

The same word is used in 1 Corinthians 12:23 to describe "our unpresentable parts," or the parts of the body that should not be presented publicly, and in Romans 1:27 to refer to the "shameful" acts of homosexuality. So to be "unseemly" means to be shameless, and it is now best translated in our modern English as to be rude or discourteous, referring to behavior that doesn't fit God's "schematic" or design or plan.

We've all seen behavior like this; indeed, we've all done it— said or done the wrong thing at the wrong time. Rude behavior is out of step, out of context, and out of order. Someone who makes a joke in a sorrowful situation is rude, so is someone who says something that is unkind. Sometimes people unintentionally do or say the wrong thing because of immaturity, lack of knowledge, or emotional stress—but that's not what I'm talking about. *Rude* refers to people who know better but choose to act out of order anyway. Paul says that *agape* love is never rude in this way. *Agape* is always thoughtful and courteous.

The New Testament commentator William Barclay translates Paul's words in verse 5 this way: "Love does not behave gracelessly." Love is gracious—it speaks and acts in a graceful manner. People are never turned off by true *agape* love, but they are definitely turned off by people who live with a lack of grace in their life. When I was helping to build a new church years ago, we did lots of door-to-door evangelism. I would occasionally get a call from someone who had been witnessed to by one of our young, zealous evangelists, asking me please not to let that person come back to their home. They had been graceless in how they presented the Gospel, and it was offensive.

Paul's words on rudeness were appropriate for the Corinthian church. There were divisions and arguments going on, they were suing one another in court, all speaking at once in worship services—they were even coming to the Lord's Supper drunk and treating it as a gluttonous feast, ignoring the poorer members of the church for whom the *agape* meal was their only source of food. They were self-centered, carnal, and offensive in many of their actions. They weren't living according to God's "schematic," or plan.

I have found three reasons for avoiding rudeness in my study of this subject. Said another way, there are three reasons for manifesting courtesy as a manifestation of *agape* love.

Courtesy Is Love's Symmetry

In 1 Corinthians 14:40, Paul's last word to the Corinthians about the conduct of their worship services, he says this: "Let all things be done decently and in order." That's the opposite of "unseemly" —it's living life according to a shape or plan. It speaks of God's order that pervades everything He does, the order by which He created the world and caused it to work "decently and in order" until sin disrupted things.

Courtesy, the opposite of rudeness, is part of the "scheme," or system, that allows us to keep our life in perspective. It helps us to know what to say and when and how to say it. Courtesy helps us take other people into account instead of focusing only on ourselves. Someone who takes pride in being outspoken, always "telling it like it is," not being afraid of stepping on others' toes—when I'm in a room with this kind of person, I know they have not internalized Paul's words about courtesy (not being rude) being a manifestation of *agape* love. Honesty and outspokenness will always be regulated by courtesy. When they are not, they become rude and offensive. Courtesy is the framework (the "scheme") that allows one to make that determination.

I have cringed upon hearing a well-meaning Christian brother or sister speak to another Christian who is going through a time of grief or suffering, announcing like a prophet exactly what that grieving person needs to do. The well-meaning one may tell the sufferer to confess and repent of the sin that brought the suffering, to have more faith, to undergo some unbiblical spiritual experience. But well-meaning doesn't excuse rude. Perhaps sin is at the root of the person's suffering. But that needs to be communicated with *agape* love, not discourteous harshness.

Courtesy is love's symmetry—it keeps virtues from becoming vices and allows a time and place and way for everything.

Courtesy Is Love's Simplicity

There's something interesting about the examples Paul mentions in 1 Corinthians 13:1-3, the huge things by which we could demonstrate our spirituality: martyrdom, speaking with tongues of men and angels, faith to move mountains, giving away our goods to feed the poor. Somehow we would rather do those huge things than the simple things that show love to our neighbor. Courtesy is love demonstrated in the little things—it is the simplicity of love.

It's so easy to overlook the simple, courteous things in life that truly say, "I love you" to another person. It was said of the Scottish poet Robert Burns, known affectionately in Scotland as "the plowman poet," that there was no truer gentleman than he. It was because he loved everything—the mouse, the daisy, and all things great and small that God had made. He was welcomed at all levels of society because of his loving temperament.

I have known outwardly simple people like this. They may not have received a higher education or wear the right clothes or be the best conversationalist. But because they had an uncomplicated, courteous spirit, they were such a pleasure to be around. That is the simplicity of true love.

The little things do make a difference when we say we love someone. Most people I have talked with would give up fancy gifts from a spouse in order to receive simple, small acts of love on a regular basis. *Agape* love means putting another person in the forefront of our thoughts and actions, thinking of them before we think of ourselves. It means doing the little things that say, "I know you and the things that mean a lot to you. I want you to know that your happiness is important to me." That's the heart of courtesy— distilling love down to its essence.

Courtesy Is Love's Sensitivity

This is probably the most important of the three points. Simply speaking, being rude or discourteous is totally incompatible with Christ being the Lord of one's life. Jesus was not rude, harsh, or biting in His relationships with people. Indeed, He was "gentle and lowly in heart" (Matthew 11:29).

John Wesley, the great Methodist preacher, was traveling in a coach with an English military officer who was intelligent and agreeable in conversation. They got along wonderfully with just one exception: The officer used very profane language. He swore continually in his conversation with Wesley. When they came to a point in their journey where they had to switch coaches, Wesley took the officer aside. He told the man how much he had enjoyed their journey together so far, and said, "I would like to ask you to do one simple favor for me, if you please."

"Certainly," the officer said. "I will take great pleasure in obliging you. You are a reasonable man who wouldn't ask me to do anything I couldn't do."

"Then," said Wesley, "since we are going to be traveling together for the next several days, I would like to ask you to promise me that, if I should forget myself and begin to swear, you will kindly reprove me immediately."

The officer got the point, and John Wesley never heard another profane word from him on their trip. That is an example of a creative and courteous solution to a difficult problem, isn't it? Our tendency might have been to dress the man down, criticize his profane language, and tell him he needed to get right with God—and lose the opportunity for any further witness or relationship in the process.

Love is courteous and graceful. If we will remember the kind of person we were before Jesus Christ changed our life, we will likely be much more patient, and more courteous, with others. It is when we adopt a "holier-than-thou" attitude toward those with whom we disagree that our rudeness hurts the cause of Christ. Love does not behave rudely.

APPLICATION

Here are some questions that will help us think about common courtesies we ought to practice. Can anyone deny that these and other graces make life more pleasant for all?

- Do you treat everyone equally, or do you snub or ignore some you deem unworthy?
- Do you respond plainly and cheerfully when spoken to, or with grunts and monosyllables?
- Do you look for ways to express kindness and courtesy to others?
- Are you courteous all the time or just when it is convenient?
- Do you show courtesy in little things more than in big things?
- Do you rush to be "first in line"?

- Men, do you hold the door open for women? Pull chairs out for when they are seated? Rise when they enter the room? Help them with their coats?
- Women, do you say "thank you" when men express these courtesies to you?
- Parents, do you model good manners and courtesy at home for your children? Do you say "please" and "thank you" to them and teach them to do the same?

We hear a lot about the "dumbing down" of modern culture from an academic perspective. But we should also be conscious of it from the perspective of courtesy. Even in Christian circles, I confess to seeing less courtesy than I used to—especially among young people and children. The danger is to believe that courtesy is a synonym for manners and that manners change with every generation. Wrong! The apostle Paul says courtesy is a synonym for love! And love never changes, never fades away, and never goes out of style—at least from God's point of view.

The Bible says that "love . . . does not behave rudely." May I encourage you today to assess your "courtesy quotient"? Don't let your love be diminished by a lack of simple kindness to others.

Note

1. Marabel Morgan, *The Electric Woman* (Waco: Word Books, 1985).

PERSONAL QUESTIONS

1. Read 1 Thessalonians 5:12-15. How would a rude person react in each situation described in these verses? In what manner do you respond in these situations? Do you act in a way that is godly?

   a. verse 12—respecting authorities:

   b. verse 13—esteeming others (note that "love" in this verse is the Greek *agape*):

   c. verse 13—pursuing peace with others:

   d. verse 14—comforting the fainthearted:

   e. verse 14—upholding the weak:

   f. verse 14—being patient with all:

   g. verse 15—responding when harmed:

   h. verse 15—pursuing what is good for self and others:

2. What doesn't love do? (1 Corinthians 13:5)

   a. What does the history of the Greek word for "unseemly" explain about what it means to "behave rudely"?

   b. What should be a priority in your relationships? (1 Corinthians 13:13) Is it?

   c. What is the worth of great things accomplished without love? (1 Corinthians 13:1-3) How is this convicting?

   d. How does *agape* relate to gracefulness?

   e. What example of a creative and courteous solution to a difficult problem is described in the lesson? What can this instance teach us about how to approach others?

   f. Have you ever found yourself with a "holier-than-thou" attitude? Toward whom? What attitude should Christians display toward others?

3. What is your estimation of the state of courtesy in our culture?

   a. What kinds of behavior are accepted today that would have been considered rude in a previous generation?

   b. How have you been affected by cultural norms of courtesy? Are you as courteous as you could or should be?

GROUP QUESTIONS

1. What three reasons for demonstrating courtesy as part of *agape* love are discussed in this chapter?

   a. Discuss the definition of courtesy as described in 1 Corinthians 14:40. What is the significance of this?

   b. What makes love's symmetry? What does courtesy help us to do? What does it prevent?

   c. Discuss love's simplicity. Why is it that, oftentimes, we would rather demonstrate our spirituality through the huge things than through simple, courteous acts of love?

   d. What are some biblical examples of simple people who accomplished great things through their love? Share ideas for small ways we can show love to those around us.

   e. What does Matthew 11:29 reveal about Jesus' attitude? What does this tell us about His love?

2. Paul's reference to love not being rude may be tied to the Corinthians' behavior at the *agape* feast. Note the kinds of behavior that might have prompted Paul's words in 1 Corinthians 11:17-22. Discuss if these attitudes are ever prevalent in Christian circles today.

   a. verses 18-19, division:

   b. verse 21, greed and self-centeredness:

   c. verses 21-22, disregard for the poor:

   d. How ironic is it that so little *agape* was present at the church's love feast? Talk about ideas on how the lack of courtesy should be (courteously) corrected if it is ever prevalent in Christian circles.

3. Read Romans 14:1-21 and discuss the following questions.

   a. What kinds of issues was the church at Rome disagreeing about? (verses 1-6)

b. How were they acting rudely toward one another? (verse 13)

c. How were they canceling out the presence of love (*agape*)? (verse 15)

d. What goals does love pursue? (verses 17, 19)

e. What is love's highest goal? (verse 21)

DID YOU KNOW?

ourteous is a Middle English term that meant "having manners fit for a royal court." The English word came by way of French *corteis* that was based on the Latin *cohors*—an enclosed yard. *Cohors* came to mean those gathered in an enclosed space, such as the courtyard of a castle or official residence. Thus, *courtesy* came to describe how one behaved in the presence of a king or other royal person—anyone deserving respect or honor (note the connection of *curtsey* as an expression of respect). By application, since all human beings bear the royal image of God (Genesis 1:26-27), there is no one not deserving of courtesy.

LOVE'S POWER OVER SELFISHNESS

1 Corinthians 13:5

*In this lesson we learn how love makes the
difference between selfishness and selflessness.*

OUTLINE

The fact that there is a magazine in our culture titled *Self* but not
one titled *Selfless* or *Others* says something about today's priorities.
Because selfless love is a rare occurrence in today's world, we know
it immediately when we see it—whether in the home, in church,
or in society.

I. **The Principle of Selflessness in the Home**

II. **The Principle of Selflessness in Service**

H ere's a sad epitaph that reportedly was found on a tombstone in a cemetery in England:

> Here lies a miser who lived for himself.
> He cared for nothing but gathering wealth.
> Now, where he is or how he fares,
> Nobody knows and nobody cares.

That is a sad testament to a life lived selfishly. Perhaps the only sadder tale is of a woman with whom Dr. W. A. Criswell had gone to visit. She was a bitter, complaining, self-centered woman who refused to receive the Gospel near the end of her life. When she died, the funeral director called Dr. Criswell and asked if he would conduct the funeral service. When he arrived at the funeral home, he discovered there was no one there except the corpse! So he conducted a funeral service that no one attended. Dr. Criswell said, in his commentary on Galatians, that this illustrated the "strangulation of selfishness" in a human life.

Contrast the record of these two lives with that on the tombstone of General Charles George Gordon in the courtyard of St. Paul's Cathedral in London:

> Sacred to the memory of General Charles George Gordon, who at all times
> and everywhere gave his strength to the weak, his substance to the poor,
> his sympathy to the suffering, and his heart to God.

We can live a selfish life or live a life with and for others—it is our choice. And selfishness is just as much a temptation for Christians as for anyone. Selfishness is part of our fallen human nature and can rear its head at any moment if we do not defend against it.

When I was a teenager, I read a tract called "Traits of the Self-Life," published by the Western Tract Mission (Saskatoon, Saskatchewan, Canada). Below is a lengthy extract from the original tract, but well worth considering in light of the theme of this lesson.

> Are you ever conscious of a secret spirit of pride, an exalted feeling in view of your success or position, because of your

good training or appearance, because of your natural gifts and abilities; an important, independent spirit, stiffness and preciseness?

Are you ever conscious of love of human praise, a secret fondness to be noticed, love of supremacy, drawing attention to self in conversation, a swelling out of self when you have had a free time in speaking or praying?

Are you ever conscious of the stirrings of anger or impatience which, worst of all, you call nervousness or holy indignation, a touchy, sensitive spirit, a disposition which dislikes being contradicted, a desire to throw sharp, heated words at another?

Are you ever conscious of self-will, a stubborn, unteachable spirit, an arguing, talkative spirit, harsh, sarcastic expressions, an unyielding, headstrong disposition, a driving, commanding spirit, a disposition to criticize and pick flaws when set aside and unnoticed, a peevish, fretful spirit, a disposition that loves to be coaxed and humored?

Are you ever conscious of a jealous disposition, a secret spirit of envy shut up in your heart, an unpleasant sensation in view of the great prosperity and success of another, a disposition to speak of the faults and failings rather than the gifts and virtues of those more talented and appreciated than yourself?

Are you ever conscious of a dishonest, deceitful disposition, the evading and covering of the truth, the covering up of your real faults, the leaving of a better impression of yourself than is strictly true, false humility, exaggeration, straining the truth?

Are you ever conscious of unbelief, a spirit of discouragement in times of pressure and opposition, lack of quietness and confidence in God, lack of faith and trust in God, a disposition to worry and complain in the midst of pain, poverty, or at the dispensations of divine providence, an overanxious feeling about whether everything will come out alright?

Are you ever conscious of formality and deadness, lack of concern for lost souls, dryness and indifference, lack of power with God? If so, you have some of the traits of the self-life.

I know I can't read that without being touched at more than one point concerning my own life—and I doubt if you read through it unscathed either. Selfishness—the self-life—happens when we fail to live lovingly toward others. Paul says that "love . . . does not seek its own" (verse 5).

This point of Paul's is probably the center point of his whole teaching on *agape* love. For the root of all human failure is the desire to have things our own way. Selfishness is the exact opposite of *agape* love. *Agape* serves others sacrificially while selfishness cares not for the needs of others. Selfishness and *agape* are at opposite ends of the scale when it comes to whom they care for the most.

We have seen how Paul's words about love were written to correct certain problems in the Corinthian church, and "does not seek its own" was no exception. They served themselves instead of others at the love feast before the Lord's Table. They were suing one another in court. They were serving themselves with the spiritual gifts they possessed, especially those who spoke in tongues, instead of serving the church. They argued about which apostle or leader they followed. They insisted on their rights to eat meat sacrificed to idols even if it caused some less mature believers to stumble in their faith.

The Corinthians were already acting the way Paul told Timothy men would act in the Last Days—they were being "lovers of themselves" (2 Timothy 3:2). The phrase "do your own thing" is typical of the perspective of many today who are looking out for "numero uno" more than anyone else. But Paul says, "That's not love!"

Selfishness and self-centeredness is at the root of most relationship problems today—marriage, parents and children, friends, coworkers. When people are out to serve their own best interests, they have little energy or love for anyone else. We certainly see this in Scripture. Lot got into trouble in Sodom because he selfishly took the best land for himself, located near Sodom, when Abraham gave him first choice (Genesis 13).

David is an example of someone who didn't seek his own. He had been anointed as the new king of Israel and could have killed Saul to get him out of the way when he had the opportunity (1 Samuel 24). But he chose not to seek his own, to wait on God's timing. And the Son of David, Jesus Christ, exemplified seeking the good of others in so many ways by taking on the form of a servant (Philippians 2). His life theme was "not My will, but Yours, be done" (Luke 22:42). Instead of forcing His disciples to serve Him, He served them by washing their feet (John 13).

The opposite of selfishness is service. You cannot live a solitary life and be selfless. Selfless people are involved in service and ministry to others. On the other hand, you cannot be a genuine servant of Christ and other people and be selfish. The more you focus on others, the less time and interest you have to focus on yourself.

Because the home is such a critical place in God's economy, it will help us to look at selflessness in that realm, followed by a look at selflessness in service to others.

THE PRINCIPLE OF SELFLESSNESS IN THE HOME

Why do athletes always say, "Hi, Mom!" when looking into a television camera? Because their moms are the unsung heroes of the home. Mothers go unrewarded and unnoticed in spite of being the backbone of the home.

Mothers have the God-given patience to wash the same dishes and clothes over and over, to tell the kids to clean their rooms over and over, and to drive the kids to the same events week after week. And many mothers who are in the work force all day have the patience to do that after working hard at a job all day. The times I have attempted to do everything my wife does in one day completely exhausted me. I could never do it like she does.

And yet, mothers keep right on coming back for more. They continue to give themselves to their children sacrificially day after day. My mother did. My wife does. And I'm sure you've seen it happen in your family as well. This version of 1 Corinthians 13, arranged specifically with mothers in mind by Diane Lorang, pictures perfectly what selflessness in the home looks like:

> If I talk to my children about what is right and what is wrong, but have not love, I am like a ringing doorbell or pots banging in the kitchen. And though I know what stages they will go through and understand their growing pains and can answer all their questions about life, and believe myself to be a devoted mother, but have not love, I am nothing. If I give up the fulfillment of a career to make my children's lives better, and stay up all night sewing costumes or making cookies on short notice, but grumble about the lack of sleep, I have not love and accomplish nothing.

A loving mother is patient with her children's immaturity, and kind even when they are not. A loving mother is not jealous of their youth nor does she hold it over their heads whenever she has sacrificed for them. A loving mother believes in her children. She hopes in each one's individual ability to stand out as a light in a dark world. She endures every backache and heartache to accomplish that. A loving mother never really dies.

As for homemade bread, it will be consumed and forgotten. As for spotless floors, they will soon gather dust and heel marks. As for children, right now, toys, friends, and food are all-important to them; but when they grow up, it will be their mother's love that they will remember and pass on to others. In that way, she will live on. So care, training, and a loving mother reside in homes, these three, but the greatest of these is a loving mother.[1]

And it's true! There, in the home, we see illustrated for us in the most beautiful way the truth that love "does not seek its own."

THE PRINCIPLE OF SELFLESSNESS IN SERVICE

Author and business consultant Tom Peters, in his book *A Passion for Excellence*, highlights a 1983 *Northwest Orient* magazine interview with Andre Saltner, chef at the Lutece restaurant in New York. What caught my eye was the connection between love and service as expressed by the chef:

I am more than thirty years as chef. I know what I am doing, and each day I do my absolute best. I cook for you from my heart with love. It must be the same with service. The waiter must serve with love. Otherwise the food is nothing. You see, many times I will leave my kitchen and go to the tables to take the orders myself. It starts right then and there; that feeling the customer must have is relaxation. If not, his evening is ruined. Mine, too, by the way. How can he love if he is not relaxed? People ask me all the time what secrets I have, and I tell them! There is nothing mysterious about Lutece. I put love in my cooking and love in my serving, and that is all.

Peters also cited Len Stephanelli, who runs a garbage business called San Francisco Sunset Scavengers: "If you don't even love your product, why would you expect people to want you to help them?" Apparently there can even be love in the garbage business!

Peters' last example was legendary Green Bay Packers' coach Vince Lombardi who once said, "Mental toughness is humility, simplicity, Spartanism, and one other—love. . . . I don't necessarily have to like my associates, but as a man, I must love them. For love is loyalty, love is teamwork, love respects the dignity of the individual. Heart power is the strength of your corporation."[2]

Love in a kitchen, a garbage company, and on the football field. If love can be the basis of those businesses, surely it can be the basis of our life as well, as we seek to minister to others in the place where God has called us.

It has been my joy over the years to write personal notes to those members of our church—and there are hundreds of them—who express their love for Christ and for others by serving as volunteer staff. Many of these dear saints I don't know personally because of the size of our church. But I definitely see the results of their service and their love.

Whether in the home or on the fields of service, people recognize *agape* love when they come in contact with it. Make sure that, wherever you are, selfless love is what people see in you.

Notes

1. Diane Lorang, "The Love Chapter for Mothers," *The Church Advocate, Volume 148*, May 1984, 10.

2. Tom Peters, *A Passion for Excellence* (New York: Warner Books, 1989), 340-341.

PERSONAL QUESTIONS

1. What did Paul mean when he said love "does not seek its own"? (1 Corinthians 13:5) In what way is *agape* an opposite characteristic of selfishness?

2. What did Paul tell Timothy men would act like in "the last days"? (2 Timothy 3:1-2)

   a. What characteristics can be tied to selfishness? Do you struggle with any of these characteristics? Turn back to the lesson and review the characteristics listed in the excerpt from the tract "Traits of the Self-Life." Have any of these traits made an appearance in your life?

   b. What are some biblical examples in which selfishness caused pain and destruction?

   c. What are some examples of times in your life when selfishness caused you pain and/or destruction? What does this show about the power of selfishness?

3. How can you take Jesus' life theme (Luke 22:42) and make it your own?

   a. If you ever find yourself becoming selfish, how can the ultimate sacrifice of Christ remind you of the true meaning of sacrificial love, and how should you act based on that?

   b. How is love connected to selflessness? Can you have one without the other?

4. When you die, what would you like to be remembered for? What legacy would you like to leave with those who knew you? If you were to die today, what would be on your epitaph? What would you be remembered for?

5. What does Philippians 2:4 exhort Christians to do?

6. What kind of world would we live in if everyone treated everything they did with love? With that in mind, how are we as Christians called to love? (John 13:35)

GROUP QUESTIONS

1. Discuss the following situations in which Christ exemplified His selflessness, and talk about how we can learn from His example.

   a. Philippians 2:5-11

   b. Luke 22:42

   c. John 13:1-17

2. Read 1 Corinthians 9:1-23 and discuss the following questions:

   a. What point about his "rights" is Paul making in the context of this passage?

   b. What posture did he take regarding his rights? (verse 15)

   c. Instead of focusing on himself (his rights), what was Paul's strategy? (verse 19) What was the purpose of his strategy? (verse 19)

d. What did Paul become to the Jews and those under the law? (verse 20)

e. How is Acts 16:1-3 an example of Paul's mindset on this issue?

f. What did Paul become to the Gentiles? (verse 21)

g. How is Acts 17:16-31 an illustration of Paul acting like a Gentile? (especially verse 28)

h. To whom is Paul referring in verse 22—the "weak"? How did Paul make the weak a priority in the church at Rome? (Romans 14:1-23)

i. Why is becoming "all things to all men" (verse 22) not an example of compromise of one's standards and beliefs?

j. Share examples of how we can set aside our own preferences in order to serve others for the sake of the Gospel.

k. Share about a time when someone was selfless toward you and how that made an impact on your life. How can true, self-sacrificial love leave a mark on someone else?

l. Talk about ways in which your group can practice selflessness in the community.

DID YOU KNOW?

A July 10, 2007, Reuters news article profiled a Malaysian hospital's efforts to persuade medical staff to wash their hands in order to cut down on disease transmission within the hospital. Warning the staff about the dangers to patients' health did not work. Installing recorded health warnings to remind staff to wash their hands pushed compliance from forty to eighty percent. Eventually, the hospital achieved success when they began pointing out the dangers to the staffs' own health (as opposed to the patients' health) by not washing their hands. The official in charge of the program said, "[Medical staff] are self-centered, not patient-centered."

LOVE'S POWER OVER ANGER

1 Corinthians 13:5

*In this lesson we discover four ways
to replace anger with love.*

OUTLINE

Society gives certain people a pass when they get angry. But Paul doesn't give anyone a pass when it comes to self-centered, sinful anger. *Agape* love and sinful anger cannot exist in the same heart.

   I. **Recover the Lost Art of Listening**

  II. **Research Your Heart**

 III. **Refuse to Seek Revenge**

 IV. **Resolve to Forgive**

Whan Pete Rose became the all-time leader in hitting in professional baseball, he broke a 57-year-old record set by a player named Ty Cobb. History records that Ty Cobb was disliked by other players with the same kind of intensity with which he played the game. He was the kind of ball player who would take out a file and put a razor edge on the metal cleats on the bottom of his baseball shoes before the game— in full view of the opposing team. It was a means of intimidation designed to make the opposing infielders nervous when he slid into a base.

Hall of Fame pitcher, Ted Lyons, said, "[Cobb] was a vicious player. He antagonized so many people that hardly anyone would even talk to him, even among his own teammates." One of Cobb's few friends, Davy Jones, said, "He had such a rotten disposition that it was hard to be his friend, and I was probably the best friend he had on this earth."[1]

By all accounts, Ty Cobb, though perhaps the greatest hitter in the history of baseball, was an angry man. He violated what the apostle Paul wrote about *agape* love: "Love . . . is not provoked." The translators of the King James Version of the Bible made a serious translation error when they rendered Paul's words this way: "Love . . . is not easily provoked." Apparently some translator couldn't believe that Paul meant that love is *never* provoked, so he inserted the word "easily" in the text to soften the requirement. But the Greek text is clear: "Love . . . is not provoked"—period!

The word *provoke* comes from two Greek words: "alongside of" and "to sharpen." Literally it meant to come alongside someone with a sharp edge so as to jab or provoke them. The opposite— not to be provoked—would mean not to respond in an angry way when jabbed or attacked. The Message says, "Love . . . doesn't fly off the handle." We sometimes excuse those who "fly off the handle," saying they are "intense" or "wired." Actually, they have a bad temper—they are allowing themselves to be provoked. And Paul says that love has no part in such a response. Because love is part of the fruit of the Holy Spirit (Galatians 5:22-23) and anger is a work of the flesh (Galatians 5:19-21), we know that love is not part of self-centered anger.

One of the greatest sermons ever preached on 1 Corinthians 13 is Henry Drummond's "The Greatest Thing in the World." Here is what he said about love not being provoked:

> No form of vice nor worldliness, nor greed of gold, nor drunkenness itself, does more to "unChristianize" society than a bad temper. For embittering life, for breaking up communities, for destroying the most sacred relationships, for devastating homes, for taking the bloom off childhood, in short, for sheer gratuitous misery-producing power, [the influence of a bad temper] stands alone.[2]

Anger, or "outbursts of wrath" as Paul calls it in Galatians 5:20, is cousin to all kinds of fleshly deeds (verses 19-21). Murder, for example, is just anger taken to its logical conclusion. If you do not check your anger, it could easily lead to the destruction of a life. This connection is reported in the news on a daily basis.

We'll look at four ways to make sure that we don't become people who are provoked, ways to make sure we manifest *agape* instead of anger.

RECOVER THE LOST ART OF LISTENING

Mark Lee, who has written a number of books on Christian marriage, has said that marriage failure is due basically to lack of communication. When people think about communication, they usually think of the talking part. But that's only half. The other half is equally important: listening. Experts say teaching people to listen is difficult but that it can be done.

I have read one estimate that says, in an average day, a person will spend 9 percent of his time writing, 16 percent reading, 30 percent speaking, and 45 percent listening. Those numbers emphasize the importance of the discipline of listening. Many people have noted that since God gave us two ears and one mouth, He must have intended for us to be twice as good at listening as we are at speaking. Strangely, awards are given for being an excellent speaker but none for being an excellent listener. Perhaps that demonstrates how undervalued listening is in our culture.

Because of our self-serving and self-centered human nature, we are always ready to talk, to tell the world what we think. Therefore, to overcome that instinct, we must develop the discipline and skill of listening. We must choose to listen. We must want to hear what the other person is saying. We must communicate love by our willingness to value the thoughts and meaning that the other person is expressing. And when it is time to respond, we must offer feedback that is helpful and relevant. Too often we listen only to earn the right to start speaking again, saying what we want to be heard and not responding at all to the other person's words.

Anger often erupts in the midst of dialogue because of what we conclude the other person has said—something that has been totally misinterpreted. The key is to seek clarification if you believe something has been said that tempts you to respond angrily: "What I am hearing you say is . . . . Is that correct? Did I misinterpret your words?"

The late Senator Sam Irvin used to talk about "Irvin's Law"—that in every verbal exchange there are three meanings: what the speaker thinks he has said, what the listener thinks the speaker has said, and what the dictionary says the speaker has said. Is it any wonder that anger erupts so easily when we try to communicate with others?

Make a commitment to be an effective listener.

RESEARCH YOUR HEART

If you are angry and have lost your *agape* love, the root of that anger is buried somewhere in your heart—and you must find it and pull it up.

The Bible warns many times about allowing oneself the luxury of being angry. We make the mistake of thinking that an outburst of anger is a momentary, isolated incident unrelated to other factors in the person's life. That is rarely the case. Anger is usually an eruption tied to something beneath the surface, and it is our job to find it—almost always with God's help in bringing things to light that need to be changed by the Holy Spirit.

The aforementioned Henry Drummond said this about the hidden sources of anger:

It is the occasional bubble that escapes to the surface and betrays some rottenness underneath, a sample of the hidden products of the soul, dropped involuntarily when one is off guard. In a word, the lightning form of a hundred hidden and unchristian sins, for want of patience, for want of kindness, for want of generosity, for want of courtesy, for want of unselfishness, all of these instantaneously are symbolized in the one flash of anger we call temper.[3]

Drummond's point is that temper is not the problem—it is but a symptom of a problem that lies beneath the surface. Someone who frequently loses his temper needs to look deeply within to discover the root cause of the symptoms.

Over the years, I have counseled with couples who experienced problems with anger in their marriage. Often the individuals were surprised to realize that it was not their spouse who was the cause of their anger, but another event or individual that represented an unresolved issue in their past—an issue that was never dealt with. Once they identified the issue(s) and dealt with it, the fuse was removed from the time bomb of their anger.

Psalm 64:6 says, "The heart of man [is] deep," and Proverbs 20:5 says, "Counsel in the heart of man is like deep water, but a man of understanding will draw it out." If you are experiencing problems with anger, I strongly encourage you to meet with a godly "man [or woman] of understanding" who can help you research your heart, identify the root cause, and help you be free from it.

REFUSE TO SEEK REVENGE

There is nothing more dangerous for a believer than to harbor the intent to "pay back" someone who has hurt you—to seek revenge. Ephesians 4:26-27 suggests that to harbor anger is to "give place to the devil." The New International Version calls this giving the devil a "foothold." The devil and his demons look for people who are angry, harboring resentment in their heart, in order to stir that anger up and encourage them to express it in hurtful ways.

Romans 12:17-21 is a classic text on dealing with revenge and attitudes toward one's enemy. Specifically, Paul says, "Repay no one evil for evil . . . . But overcome evil with good." To seek revenge is to put anger in motion and to disobey God in the process. When Jesus was attacked, He did not attack in return (1 Peter 2:23). By staying free from sin, He stayed free from the control or influence of Satan in His life—and the same will be true of you and me. But to yield to anger and the temptation to revenge is to go over to the dark side, to give way to the impulses of the flesh that the devil loves to empower.

Do not give in to the temptation to seek revenge. *Agape* is only found in loving our neighbor as ourself (Matthew 22:39).

RESOLVE TO FORGIVE

If there is a consistent root buried in the heart of those who struggle with anger, it is the root of unforgiveness. If you have something in your heart against another person, then you can justify or rationalize your anger. If you have forgiven the other person and have nothing festering in your heart, then you have no grounds for anger. So unforgiveness is often the common denominator among those who are angry toward another person.

A very helpful book by the late Lewis Smedes, *Forgive and Forget*, deals with some unhelpful misconceptions that have been perpetuated about forgiveness.[4] Christians are often told that if you haven't forgotten another's sin against you, you haven't forgiven the sin. Smedes points out that forgiving and forgetting are not always simultaneous. Sins against us often scar us for life, and they are not always immediately forgotten even if we have forgiven the person for the offense. Neuroscience tells us that the human brain stores every event in life. Some events gradually fade from memory; but others do not, depending on their emotional intensity, how often the memory is refreshed, and other factors.

"Forgiving and forgetting" doesn't mean that we actually lose all cognitive traces of the hurtful event. It means, "I forgive you, and I choose not to hold that event against you. I choose to act toward you as if the event had never happened, even though my memory tells me it did."

Lewis Smedes tells the story of Simon Wiesenthal and his own terrible crisis of forgiveness in a Nazi concentration camp in World War II.

Wiesenthal was a Jew interred in a Polish concentration camp who was brought to the bedside of a young, wounded German soldier in the camp hospital. The soldier was desperate to talk to a Jew—to confess the terrible things he had done against the Jewish people so he could be forgiven and die in peace. The sin that burdened his soul was having participated in the burning alive of a group of about two hundred Jews who had been forced into a house which was then set ablaze. The soldier said to Wiesenthal, "I know that what I have told you is terrible. I have longed to talk about it to a Jew and beg forgiveness of him. I know that what I am asking is almost too much, but without your answer, I cannot die in peace." Without a word Wiesenthal turned and walked out of the room, leaving the man to die in his unforgiven state.

Wiesenthal survived the concentration camp but was haunted for years about what he had done. He even told the story in a book years later, asking his readers, "What would you have done?"

He received letters from all over the world from people telling him what they would have done and what they thought he should have done.

The greater question for every Christian is, what would *you* have done? Having been forgiven by God for all our sins, could we ever justify withholding forgiveness from another?

If you want to be free of anger, you must learn to listen, search your heart, set aside vengeance, and resolve to forgive everyone for everything. Only then will you be free.

Notes

1. Michael Hartley, *Christy Mathewson: A Biography* (Jefferson: McFarland, 2004), 95.

2. Henry Drummond, *The Greatest Thing in the World* (New York: Fleming H. Revell Company, 1898), 6.

3. Ibid.

4. Lewis B. Smedes, *Forgive and Forget* (San Francisco: Harper and Row, 1984), 127.

1. What is the meaning of the word "provoked" in 1 Corinthians 13:5?

   a. What does Galatians 5:19-21 say about those who practice "outbursts of wrath"?

   b. Why does the Bible warn us about being angry?

   c. What is wrath, or anger, tied to? (What is the source of it?) What can it lead to?

2. What does Ephesians 4:26-27 say about revenge, or "payback"? Why is harboring resentment dangerous? What does it allow the devil to do?

   a. What is the risk of unforgiveness? What does the Bible tell us about forgiveness? (Mark 11:25; Ephesians 4:32; Matthew 18:21-22; Matthew 6:14-15)

   b. Can you distinguish the difference between forgiving and forgetting? Why is it important to differentiate the two?

3. In the story about the Nazi concentration camp soldier, what would you have done if you had been Wiesenthal? How does your response compare to Wiesenthal's?

4. Read James 1:19-20.

   a. What is an essential part of communication that people oftentimes overlook? Are you good at practicing this necessary factor?

   b. Why is being an effective listener important? How can you work on this skill in your life?

   c. What advice do you find in verse 19 about the discipline of listening?

   d. What does "slow to wrath" suggest about anger being a matter of choice? (verse 19) How are being "swift to hear" and "slow to wrath" related?

   e. What does the "wrath of man" not produce? (verse 20) Try to write this verse out in your own words to clarify what you think it means in practical terms.

5. What likelihood increases the more one talks? (Proverbs 10:19)

6. Therefore, why is there wisdom in holding one's tongue?

7. What do we learn from Proverbs 17:27 about a man who limits his words?

   a. What kind of temper does such a man have?

   b. Does using few words produce an even temper or vice versa?

1. What is the meaning of the word "provoked" in 1 Corinthians 13:5?

2. List and discuss the four ways this lesson tells us we can become people who are not easily provoked.

   •

   •

   •

   •

3. What is an essential part of communication that people oftentimes overlook? In your group, discuss why this might be true.

4. Expand on the value of listening. How can speaking too much and not listening be self-serving?

5. Why is being an effective listener important?

6. How can we become better listeners?

7. Discuss what Jeremiah 17:9 says about the (natural, fallen) human heart.

a. What did David ask God to show him about his own heart? (Psalm 139:23-24) How can we learn from this?

b. What does David's request suggest about our ability to know our own heart?

c. Share what you have learned about your heart that you didn't know until God showed it to you.

d. Why does God sometimes allow us to undergo tests and temptations? (Psalm 26:2; Proverbs 17:3)

8. Read Romans 12:18-21.

a. Who bears the responsibility for living at peace with others? (verse 18) Discuss whether this peace is common in Christian circles or not.

b. What should we do for one who is provoking us? (verse 20) Share ideas on how we can train ourselves to be patient when someone is provoking us.

c. How can verse 21 encourage us in that?

9. Explain what Jesus meant regarding forgiveness in Matthew 6:14-15.

a. In light of that verse, are any of our sins in danger of not being forgiven? Do we have a right, as Christians, to withhold our forgiveness from anyone?

b. How is Paul saying essentially the same thing in Ephesians 4:32?

DID YOU KNOW?

First Corinthians contains ample evidence for why Paul wrote that "love . . . is not provoked." In chapter 6 Paul notes that the believers were suing one another over disputes that they couldn't settle themselves. Then in chapter 7, he instructs believers not to separate from their marriage partners but to remain married. This suggests that divorce was an issue in the church. Then in chapter 8, some less mature believers were apparently provoked by other believers' willingness to eat meat that had been sacrificed to pagan idols. And poor people in the church were no doubt provoked by how they were ignored at the church's love feast before celebrating the Lord's Supper.

LOVE'S POWER OVER RESENTMENT

1 Corinthians 13:5

*In this lesson we learn how to live free
from the debilitating power of resentment.*

OUTLINE

Just as giant wild fires are often started from one careless spark, so raging fires of anger often begin by not dealing with small resentments when they occur. Resentments are the records of wrongs we have suffered. Failing to erase them from the ledger will put us in a deficit of love.

   I. The Examination of Resentment

  II. The Example of Resentment

 III. The Expense of Resentment

 IV. The Excising of Resentment
     A. Think It Through
     B. Write It Down
     C. Work It Out
     D. Talk It Over
     E. Give It Up

One January day in 1984, Pope John Paul II made his way to a cell in the Rebibbia prison in Rome. There he met with Mehmet Ali Agca, the man who had fired a bullet into his chest in an attempt to assassinate him. Taking his would-be assassin's hand, the pope forgave him.

We have to be impressed with the pope's act of forgiveness—it must not have been an easy thing to do. Yet I believe it is multiple times more difficult for an average, unknown person like you or me to forgive those who harm us than it is when the world's spotlight is trained on a person and he is expected to forgive. Yet, difficult as it may be, Paul says in 1 Corinthians 13:5 that love forgives—that is, it keeps no record of wrongs experienced.

We'll focus our study of forgiveness on four aspects of resentment—since we cannot embrace resentment and forgive at the same time. If we are going to truly forgive, resentment has to be released.

THE EXAMINATION OF RESENTMENT

The phrase in the KJV and the NKJV of the Bible—"thinks no evil"—is not the best translation of the Greek word *logizomai*. That word means "to think or to take into account"—an accounting or bookkeeping term. We enter numbers into a spreadsheet in order to make a permanent copy of them which can be examined at a future date. That is exactly what we don't want to do when it comes to personal relationships—keep a permanent record of them for consulting in the future. Therefore, "love . . . keeps no record of wrongs" (verse 5, NIV) is a better translation.

Logizomai is used in similar ways in other places in the New Testament. Romans 4:8 says the man is blessed to whom the Lord does not impute (*logizomai*, add to his personal record; keep track of) sin. Second Corinthians 5:19 has a similar use of the word where God does not impute (*logizomai*, add to their permanent record) man's sins to him. And Philippians 4:8 says we should "meditate on" (*logizomai*, think about, calculate, keep track of) virtuous and noble and pure ideas.

What is resentment if not the writing down (figuratively or literally) and keeping track of the wrongs we have suffered? And Paul says that people who love do not keep track of wrongs suffered. Instead, they forgive.

Anger and resentment are coupled this way: Resentment simmers beneath the surface and then finally boils over in a display of anger. The ledger book gets so full of recorded wrongs that you finally express your anger at being treated badly. When offenses are not forgiven immediately, they become like logs and trees that accumulate in a creek and eventually stop the flow of water.

The Church father, Chrysostom, wrote, "A wrong done against love should be like a spark that falls into the sea and is quenched. Love quenches wrongs rather than recording them. It does not cultivate memories out of evils. If God so completely and permanently erases the record of our many sins against Him, how much more should we forgive and forget the much lesser wrongs done against us? Love doesn't keep track of everything that has happened. Love forgives, love dismisses, love goes on."

THE EXAMPLE OF RESENTMENT

An unusual case of resentment—long-held resentment—is revealed in the closing words of King David to his son and successor, Solomon (1 Kings 2:1-9). His words were positive and uplifting until we get to verse 5 where he brings up the deeds of Joab, the commander of his armies, and a man named Shimei who had been a political enemy of David. David commissioned Solomon to end both men's lives because of what they had done against David.

In Shimei's case, David had promised not to harm the man as long as he (David) was alive. But as soon as he died, David wanted the man dispatched quickly. David was a man after God's heart, yet even he succumbed to the temptation of resentment, the failure to forgive those who had wronged him. Who knows what personal toll that resentment took on his life.

THE EXPENSE OF RESENTMENT

In his book *None of These Diseases,* Dr. M. I. McMillen says, "Medical science recognizes that emotions such as fear, sorrow, envy, resentment, and hatred are responsible for the majority of our sicknesses. Estimates vary from 60 percent to nearly 100 percent."[1]

Resentment is so very destructive. Lewis Smedes, whose book on forgiveness I quoted in the previous lesson, wrote in that same book, "We make believe that we are at peace while the furies rage within beneath the surface. There, hidden and suppressed, our hate opens the subterranean faucets of venom that will eventually infect all our relationships in ways we cannot predict. Hate left to itself, denied and hidden, leaves us in a cold hell behind insulated masks of warm friendship."[2]

There are people in this life who have been hurt by others but who have maintained a relationship with that person. Perhaps a wife who was left by her husband or vice versa. They are willing to maintain a civil relationship with that person, but the one thing they won't do is release the resentment for what that person did to them. They would rather be eaten up on the inside with resentment than forgive the person for what they did. It's a terrible price to pay, but many people do it. I encourage you not to be one of them.

THE EXCISING OF RESENTMENT

Just as a surgeon takes his scalpel and excises a tumor from deep within a patient, so we must take whatever steps are needed to get the resentment out of our heart. The following five steps can lead you to freedom if you will follow them.

Think It Through

The first step is a mental one—an exercise in reason: Why would anyone want to keep a black hole of resentment and hatred down deep inside? Given the cost of harboring resentment, it doesn't make sense to embrace it—but people do anyway. Here are some reasons why people do what is unreasonable.

First, resentment makes us feel superior to the one we resent. We think of ourselves as the good person who was harmed by the bad person, and it makes us feel better about ourselves.

Second, resentment allows us to indulge our minds in the fantasy of revenge. Everyone has had the experience of being in a conflict and then later thinking of things we wish we'd said. It's the same with fantasies of revenge—we create elaborate plots for how we'll get back at the person who harmed us. There is a measure of perverse pleasure in such exercises that our flesh enjoys.

Third, resentment allows you to punish yourself. In a twisted way, resentment allows the "resenter" to punish himself for doing something he knows is wrong. Resentment makes us feel bad, depressed, and discouraged; and feeling that bad makes us feel less bad about harboring the resentment in the first place. So you rehearse what the person did to you with anyone who will listen. The more you retell your story, the worse you feel, and the more punished you feel. Does this make logical sense? No, but the human psyche is not always about what makes sense.

If you will think it through on these three fronts, you'll find that resentment is not a good investment of your mental, spiritual, emotional, and physical energy.

Write It Down

One of the best ways to deal objectively with your resentment is to write down why you are resentful. At the top of a piece of paper write "Why I Am Filled With Resentment." Then write down the reasons. Don't overstate or understate them, just write down the factual reasons as best you can. Then spend some time looking at what you've written. Taken out of the emotional realm of your inner person and put on a piece of paper in black and white, your reasons will look less ominous. They will not look as angry as you feel. You may even discover that your mind has been playing tricks on you, that you are less resentful than you thought you were.

Writing it down is a form of venting that can help. Author Charlie Shedd came into the kitchen the day after he and his wife had had a big fight and found a note taped to the counter. It said, "Dear Charlie, I hate you. Love, Martha." Writing it down helped her be honest about what she was thinking and feeling—in a humorous way.

Work It Out

One of the best ways to work out the stress and tension that resentment creates is through physical exercise. Tennis, racquetball, jogging, biking—whatever lets you work out your aggression without directing it toward a person will help you.

Donna and I knew a couple when we were in seminary who became our good friends. The wife had a difficult time with her temper, so whenever she was upset with her husband, her outlet was to rearrange the furniture. Whenever we visited in their home, we could tell how well they had been getting along because of the way the house looked!

A man who had been married to his wife for fifty years revealed the secret of their longevity: "The wife and I had an agreement when we first got married. The agreement was, when she was bothered about something, she would just tell me off and get it out of her system. And if I was mad at her about something, I was to take a walk. I suppose you could attribute our marital success to the fact that I have largely led an outdoor life."

Talk It Over

If you have a friend who will let you pour out your heart, resentment and all, without judging you—but without sympathizing with you either—you have a great friend. I do not mean that friends should be used by you to talk about what others have done to you. But sometimes it will help to admit that you are struggling with resentment and get what counsel and prayer you can from a friend. The best friends are those who will say, "You know, it sounds to me like you might be overreacting. I think you ought to back off and take a fresh look at this before you become trapped in your resentment." The loving wounds of this kind of friend can be a gentle rebuke when needed and keep us from devolving into a place of serious sin.

If marriage partners could learn to talk over their disagreements and hurts according to Paul's prescription in Ephesians 4:25-26 (speak the truth; don't let the sun go down on your anger), they would do themselves a great service. If small sparks could be extinguished within 24 hours of their ignition, they would never have the opportunity to become the raging fires that happen when resentments build up over time. Sadly, because marriage partners haven't kept the ledgers clean for so long, there is already so much resentment that they can't sit down and talk about today's events.

One married couple said they had decided early in their marriage to follow Paul's prescription not to go to sleep without dealing with any issues between them. "Of course," they said, "we had lots of sleepless nights, but at least we kept our word."

Give It Up

The church I pastored years ago in the Midwest was making an addition to the church campus, and the masonry crew worked for a period right outside the window of my study. Those guys fought like cats and dogs all day, using language I was not used to hearing. But the next morning, they would show up, laughing and carrying on, and go right back to work. And I thought, how much more should Christians, who have the power of the Holy Spirit, do the same thing after an argument?

I have read that a friend of Clara Barton, who was the founder of the American Red Cross, once reminded her of an especially cruel thing that someone had done to her years before. Miss Barton couldn't remember what it was. "Don't you remember," her friend said. "No," Barton said, "I distinctly remember forgetting it."[3]

You may never completely forget about a wrong done to you, but you can choose not to let it hinder your relationship with the other person. The Scottish theologian, H. R. MacIntosh, put it this way: "Forgiveness is an active process of the mind and temper of a wronged person by means of which he abolishes the moral hindrance to fellowship with the wrongdoer and establishes the freedom and the happiness of a friendship." That's a formal way of saying, "Give it up. Get over it. Put it behind you."

Notes

1. S. I. McMillen, *None of These Diseases* (Grand Rapids: Fleming H. Revell, 1963).

2. Lewis B. Smedes, *Forgive and Forget* (San Francisco: Harper and Row, 1984).

3. Alan Loy McGinnis, *The Friendship Factor* (Minneapolis: Augsburg Books, 2004), 168.

PERSONAL QUESTIONS

1. What does the phrase "thinks no evil" mean in 1 Corinthians 13:5? What does the history of the translation of this phrase reveal about its true meaning?

2. How does resentment compare to anger? What is the difference?

3. How can feelings of resentment affect your life?

4. How does love respond to being wronged?

5. Is forgiveness easy? How is it possible?

6. Do you struggle with feelings of anger or bitterness? What is the root of your anger? How can these feelings be destructive?

7. Is there anyone who has wronged you that you have not yet forgiven?

8. According to the lesson, what are five steps that can lead you to freedom from resentment? If you harbor any feelings of resentment toward anyone, take these steps toward ridding yourself of these destructive feelings.

9. What does Romans 12:17-21 say about responding to the feeling of revenge? How does Jesus' example in 1 Peter 2:23 further enforce this idea? If Jesus forgave you, do you have any right to be unforgiving toward others?

10. Read Hebrews 12:14-15.

   a. What is the believer's responsibility as far as peace with others is concerned? (verse 14)

   b. If you have been hurt by someone, what would pursuing peace look like? How would you do it?

11. In general terms, what principle does Matthew 18:15 set forth for pursuing peace with others?

12. If you know that someone is resentful toward you, what should you do? (Matthew 5:23-24)

13. How might the behavior described in Romans 12:20 help to defuse resentment in another person?

1. What does "thinks no evil" mean in 1 Corinthians 13:5? Discuss what the history of the translation of this phrase tells us about its true meaning.

2. How should the truth be spoken? (Ephesians 4:15)

   a. How is it possible to do this without being condescending? Talk through examples of ways to speak "truth in love."

   b. How is truth-speaking a corrective for those who are acting like children? (verse 14)

   c. How do children act when they have been hurt by another? How common is it to find this behavior in Christian circles?

d. What do adults do when they are hurt and act like children instead of grown-ups? (verse 15)

e. Have you ever found yourself acting childishly when reprimanded by a brother or sister in Christ? How can we learn to accept correction humbly?

f. Talk about the appropriate reaction we should have toward a reprimand given in love.

3. How do Ephesians 4:15 and 4:25-26 work together to keep us from giving the devil a foothold in a relationship?

4. Read 2 Corinthians 5:18-20 and discuss the following questions:

a. What ministry has God given to every Christian? (verse 18)

b. What did God not count against men in order for reconciliation with Himself to take place? (verse 19)

c. What does Paul call Christians in verse 20? Do we take this seriously in the way we live our life?

d. Whom, in your community, can you be an ambassador to? How?

DID YOU KNOW?

A farmer, visiting a friend in the country, was leaning on a fence watching an old farmer plowing a field. The farmer's mule seemed confused about what the farmer was trying to get him to do. The visitor spoke up: "I hope you don't think I'm telling you how to run your business, but you could save yourself a lot of time and energy if you'd just say 'Giddyap' and 'Whoa,' and 'Gee' and 'Haw' to your mule instead of just tugging on those reins." The old farmer stopped the mules, drew a handkerchief from his pocket and wiped his face, and said, "You're right. But this mule stepped on my foot five years ago, and I haven't spoken to him since."

LOVE'S POWER OVER A NEGATIVE ATTITUDE

1 Corinthians 13:6

In this lesson we learn the dangers of rejoicing in unrighteousness.

OUTLINE

Christians have tried to sanctify a certain sin by engaging in "sharing": "I need to share this with you about so-and-so." There is nothing loving about taking pleasure in the sins or difficulties of others, but there is something sinful about it. We are to rejoice in what edifies, and nothing else.

I. A Sin Against God

II. A Subtle Temptation

III. A Synonym for Gossip

There is very little in life that we can change. But the one thing we have absolute control over is how we respond to everything else. While we may feel powerless when it comes to what happens in the world around us, we do have power over our responses to the things we can't change. And that truth is at the heart of Paul's words in 1 Corinthians 13:6: "[Love] does not rejoice in iniquity, but rejoices in the truth."

Early in 1939, the Spanish Civil War was almost over. Outside Madrid, a rebel by the name of General Mola prepared to attack. Someone asked him which of his four columns would be the first to enter the city. To the inquirer's surprise the general said, "Not any of the four. It will be the fifth." General Mola was speaking of the most important force he knew that would help him win his battle: the rebel sympathizers who were already in the city. A part of the community he was trying to defeat was already fighting for him behind Loyalist lines.

General Mola's remark coined the phrase "fifth column activity," and it has become a synonym for traitorous forces in times of war. During World War II, it was a fifth column in Norway that brought about the country's collapse. Norway's leader, Vidkun Quisling, became a puppet premier of Adolf Hitler and the German Nazis. And when Norway was freed at the end of the war, Quisling was put to death for treason.

There is fifth column activity in the Church. Satan has a fifth column: the people of God who haven't learned how to rejoice in the truth. Instead, they spend all their time rejoicing in iniquity.

When Paul wrote that love "does not rejoice in iniquity," he meant that love takes no satisfaction in sin. It's bad enough to commit sins, but taking satisfaction in sin by talking or joking about it has no place in the life of love. To rejoice in unrighteousness is to glorify it, to make it appear that wrong is right. The prophet Isaiah warned about such an attitude when he wrote, "Woe to those who call evil good, and good evil; who put darkness for light, and light for darkness; who put bitter for sweet, and sweet for bitter!" (Isaiah 5:20)

There is much rejoicing in iniquity in our world. Crime and violence have become the most popular forms of entertainment on television and in movies. Bad news is good news when it comes to making headlines and selling ad space on TV. People have an insatiable appetite for the unsavory and the unrighteous, but tragedy or misfortune in any form is a cause for sadness with God.

The danger, even for Christians, is to find ourselves inwardly glad when another's misfortune results in a benefit for us. There is no love when we feign sorrow on the outside but rejoice on the inside.

Third John 4 says, "I have no greater joy than to hear that my children walk in truth." Righteousness and truth should be the source of our rejoicing. When we hear that others are doing well, we should rejoice in their blessing. And when others fail or sin? Peter's words are appropriate: "And above all things have fervent love for one another, for 'love [agape] will cover a multitude of sins'" (1 Peter 4:8). When someone sins or struggles, agape love covers their sins. We don't broadcast another's sins or misfortunes. Instead, we reach out selflessly to bring in the wounded one and restore him or her.

When Noah became drunk on one occasion and was lying down asleep and uncovered, his sons Shem and Japheth took a garment and, holding it between them, backed toward their father and covered his nakedness. They didn't rejoice in their father's failure but maintained their love and respect for him, and preserved his dignity by covering him (Genesis 9:20-23). That's a good example of what Paul is talking about in 1 Corinthians 13:6—not rejoicing in iniquity.

I have actually known of marriage partners who hoped their spouse would commit adultery so the "innocent" partner would have grounds for divorce. Or perhaps someone hopes that a coworker will be found to be dishonest or unethical so he won't be promoted, making the other person more likely to get the promotion. We should never hope for harm for anyone! There is no love in such hopes.

There are three primary reasons we should never rejoice in unrighteousness or iniquity.

A SIN AGAINST GOD

First, rejoicing in evil is a sin against God, an affront to that which God considers right and just. To take pleasure in sin is to take pleasure in something that offends the heart of God. We are finding satisfaction in the very thing that caused Jesus Christ to be nailed to the cross. Can you imagine standing at the foot of the cross and rejoicing with a friend about someone else's misfortune or sin? It's a ludicrous thought—but when we take any view of sin contrary to God's, we mock the death that Christ died.

A SUBTLE TEMPTATION

You may not yet have found a way to connect with the theme of this message. After all, you don't rejoice in another person's sins or in society's sins. But there are other subtle ways that you can be tempted to rejoice in another's misfortune.

If a college student is struggling to make a *B* in a difficult class, he may take inner satisfaction when others receive a *C*. He may be secretly rejoicing, not that he did so well but that others did so poorly. It's tempting to rejoice at others' problems when they make you look good.

Or if you're a businessman or woman and your company has fallen on hard times, you probably will feel badly, especially if your competitors are succeeding. It's tempting to rejoice on the day you hear that they have fallen on hard times as well.

What about you who are parents? If your children are going through a difficult time and causing you no end of embarrassment, you hate it if your friends' children are sailing through life without any problems. And if one of those children stumbles, you are tempted to rejoice at the fact that you are not the only parent with imperfect children.

And it can happen in the ministry. Pastors, leaders, and others can be disheartened when their work appears not to be bearing fruit. And they can be tempted to draw encouragement (in a twisted way) when other ministries falter along with their own.

Do you see how subtle these temptations can be? If we are not careful, we will find ourselves rejoicing in the misfortune, if not the outright sins, of others. Instead, we ought to be covering our friends with love—reaching out to do what we can to encourage them and help them in their difficult time.

A Synonym for Gossip

Participating in gossip—as a speaker or listener—is often a way to rejoice in evil or the misfortune of others. Plainly speaking, gossip is sin. Some people believe that if what they are saying or hearing is true, it's not gossip. Wrong! Gossip is gossip, whether what is said is true or false.

Bad news travels on the grapevine—even the Christian grapevine —much faster than good news. When someone says, "Did you hear about . . . ?" it's usually some kind of bad news or juicy tidbit that amounts to gossip. Spreading bad news via gossip is the epitome of rejoicing in iniquity, misfortune, or unrighteousness.

I love what Ephesians 4:29 says: "Let no unwholesome word proceed from your mouth, but only such a word as is good for edification according to the need of the moment, so that it will give grace to those who hear" (NASB1995). Someone has estimated that the average person utters some thirty thousand words every day. Compare that with Proverbs 10:19: "In the multitude of words sin is not lacking, but he who restrains his lips is wise."Somewhere in the multitude of words we speak each day lies the potential for great sin by speech.

The great danger with gossip is that once the words are spoken, they are gone—there is no accounting for the damage they might do after you spoke them. A Christian couple who are known in many Christian circles battled the consequences of a rumor started about them that they were about to divorce. Nothing was further from the truth! Yet it had a terrible impact on their lives and ministry. They finally tracked the source of the rumor down to one individual who repeated something he had heard that was not true. When you spread gossip, it is like a new strain of virus that replicates itself and may never be stopped.

The book of Proverbs speaks often about the use of words, and two themes emerge (among others). First, it is wrong to be a gossip; and second, it is dangerous to associate with one. Not only should you not spread truth or lies about others that highlights their misfortune or sin, you shouldn't listen to it either. The danger in hanging around anyone is the possibility of becoming like that person. So if you participate in gossip by listening, you are more likely to become a gossip yourself. Do you realize that without someone to listen, a gossip is stopped cold in his or her tracks (Proverbs 26:20)? Don't be the listener, and for sure don't be the speaker.

The great English Methodist preacher, John Wesley, established a covenant for himself and for all the lay preachers he worked with in his ministry. He required every man who ministered with him to agree to, and sign, the covenant—and to hang it on a wall in their home so they would continually be reminded of it. Here are the six points of the covenant:

1. That we will not listen to, or willingly inquire after, ill concerning one another.

2. That if we do hear any ill of each other, we will not be forward to believe it.

3. That as soon as possible, we will communicate what we hear by speaking or writing to the person concerned.

4. That until we have done this, we will not write or speak a syllable of it to any other person.

5. That neither will there be mention of it after we have done this to any other person.

6. That we will not make any exception to any of these rules unless we think ourselves absolutely obliged in conference.

They agreed not to believe nor repeat any untoward thing they heard about one of their brothers until they had checked it out with the brother himself. What a difference such a covenant and accompanying practice would make in the Church of Jesus Christ! Our commitment would be to love, not to the bad report we might hear about another brother or sister in Christ. You and I can choose what we rejoice in and what we tell others. As I said at the beginning of this lesson, there is much in this world we cannot control, but we can control what we choose to say and listen to.

One of the best illustrations of gossip I ever heard came from the Christian businessman R. G. LeTourneau, famous for his design of massive earth-moving and construction machines. He had one giant earthmover that he called "The G Machine." When someone asked him why he named it The G Machine, he explained that the G stood for "gossip." "This machine has the same capabilities as gossip," he said. "It can move lots of dirt fast." You and I don't want to be "G Machines," moving dirt around in the Christian community (or our neighborhoods or anywhere else).

Near the end of the sixteenth century, a famous French preacher by the name of Bishop Massillon had some strong comments concerning the apostle James' teaching about the power of the tongue:

> The tongue of a slanderer is a devouring fire which tarnishes whatever it touches, which exercises its fury on the good and on the evil, on the profane and on the sacred; which, wherever it passes leaves only desolation and ruin. . . . It is disguised hatred which sheds the hidden venom of the heart, and unworthy duplicity which praises to the face, and then tears to pieces behind the back, a shameful levity which often sacrifices both fortune and comfort to the imprudence of an amusing conversation. . . . It is a restless evil which disturbs society, spreads dissension through cities and countries, disunites the strictest friendships. It is the source of hatred and revenge, and everywhere is an enemy to peace, comfort and Christian good breeding.[1]

That is a straightforward and eloquent description of rejoicing in iniquity! It is a sin against God, a subtle temptation, and a synonym for gossip—always to be avoided!

Note

1. J. B. Massillon, Bishop of Clermont, *Sermons by J. B. Massillon* (M. Carey and Son, 1818), 165-167.

PERSONAL QUESTIONS

1. Although we oftentimes have no control over our situation, over what do we have control?

   a. What does Paul mean when he says that love "does not rejoice in iniquity"? (1 Corinthians 13:6) How does this tie into Isaiah 5:20?

   b. Although we may not wish sorrow upon another person, sometimes we are tempted to hope they won't do their best so we don't look so bad. Have you ever been guilty of this?

   c. How do you feel when another's misfortune results in a benefit for you? Is your reaction biblical?

   d. How can our own misery lead to resentment toward others? Is it rooted in jealousy or envy?

2. Based on the discussion in the lesson, what are two themes Proverbs highlights about the topic of gossip?

   • It is wrong to . . .

   • It is dangerous to . . .

   a. What can happen when we hang around someone that may be a bad influence?

b. How can Ephesians 4:29 be convicting in relation to the topic of gossip?

3. Is gossiping a sin? Why?

   a. Do you ever find yourself participating in gossip?

   b. How can we cut out this bad habit from our life?

4. What does Proverbs 10:19 say about holding our tongue? What can we learn from this?

5. How much power do our words hold?

   a. What damage can they cause to someone else?

   b. How might this encourage us to think before we speak?

6. Can gossip add to the negativity in our life?

   a. What can be some effects of that?

   b. How can we stop gossip? (Proverbs 26:20)

7. How can we learn to rejoice in the truth?

GROUP QUESTIONS

1. Discuss what Paul meant when he said that love "does not rejoice in iniquity." (1 Corinthians 13:6)

   a. How does this description tie into what is stated in Isaiah 5:20?

   b. List and discuss the three reasons we should never rejoice in unrighteousness.

      •

      •

      •

2. As a group, discuss how gossip and participating in bad reports contribute to the possibility of schism in the Body of Christ. (1 Corinthians 12:25)

   a. Why are those activities inconsistent with members having "the same care for one another"? (1 Corinthians 12:25)

   b. If someone suffers (for whatever reason), what should the rest of the Church do? (1 Corinthians 12:26; Romans 12:15)

   c. What does it mean to "suffer with" someone?

   d. What is the image presented in Hebrews 13:3 concerning the corporate nature of the Body of Christ?

3. If every member is joined together (Ephesians 4:16), what is the implication when we rejoice in another's sin or misfortune?

   a. How is one's misfortune the misfortune of all?

   b. What did Job say he had done upon hearing of others' misfortune? (Job 30:25) How can we learn from his reaction?

4. Answer and discuss the following questions based on the verses in Proverbs:

   a. To what does the "mouth of the foolish" lead? (10:14)

   b. The more we talk, the more we are likely to _____. (10:19) Why is this?

   c. If we are wise, we will _____. (10:19)

   d. What does a gossip do? (11:13)

   e. What does a faithful person do? (11:13)

   f. Whom do we protect when we watch what we say? (13:3)

   g. What can a "whisperer" do by his actions? (16:28)

   h. What should be our response to a gossip? (20:19)

   i. Explain the metaphors used in Proverbs 25:19 to illustrate the dangers of an unfaithful person.

   j. If we cannot control our tongue, what are we like? Explain the metaphor in Proverbs 25:28.

   k. What is the quickest way to put out the fire of gossip? (26:20)

DID YOU KNOW?

Etymologist John Ayto (*Dictionary of Word Origins*) says that the English word *gossip* comes from the Anglo-Saxon *godsibb*, the word for "godparent" (*god* = god, *sib* = relative). A *godsibb* was one's "relative in God" or "spiritual relative." By the time of Middle English, a godsibb had become simply a "close friend." By the 16th century a godsibb had become what we know as a gossip —a person who did what close friends often do: engage in idle chatter. The spelling evolved over time to become our word *gossip*, referring to the person and the activity. True "spiritual relatives" do not engage in idle chatter that could result in harm to others.

LOVE'S POWER OVER DISCOURAGEMENT

1 Corinthians 13:7

In this lesson we learn how love is a shield against life's unknowns.

OUTLINE

Some people are optimists; some are pessimists; some are realists; some are idealists; some are cynics; some are positive. But the people who are the most positive and appealing to others are those filled with love. Love knows how to handle and understand everything life brings.

I. The Protection of Love
   A. Love Is a Retreat That Shelters From the Storms of Life
   B. Love Is a Relationship That Sympathizes With the Sorrows of Life
   C. Love Is a Response That Submits to the Slights of Life

II. The Possibility of Love
   A. Hope Never Allows Facts to Be Forgotten
   B. Hope Never Allows Failure to Be Final

III. The Patience of Love

Everybody has a way of responding when life doesn't go as expected or as planned. But the apostle Paul was convinced that one thing was sufficient to sustain us through all of life's events: *agape* love. He wrote in 1 Corinthians 13:7, "[Love] bears all things, believes all things, hopes all things, endures all things."

This verse expands our understanding of the nature of love. Love isn't just for marriage, family, or other relationships. By his four-fold use of the word "all," Paul says that love is the sustaining foundation for all of life. Love touches every part of life and can provide a framework for interpreting all of life's events.

Four verses of Scripture give us the theological understanding we need to rightly interpret "all":

- Romans 8:28 says God causes *all* things to work together for good for those who love God.
- Romans 11:36 says *all* things are of Him and through Him and to Him.
- Ephesians 1:11 says God works *all* things according to the counsel of His will.
- Revelation 4:11 says God created *all* things according to His will.

In summary, God is the cause, center, controller, and creator of all things—including the unexpected and unplanned things in our life. God doesn't cause evil or sin; but in His position as the controller of all things, He allows room for bad things to happen for His ultimate purposes. When we understand these theological truths, we can better understand Paul's words in 1 Corinthians 13:7.

THE PROTECTION OF LOVE

The word for "bears" in verse 7 has two meanings in the Greek New Testament. It can mean "to support from beneath, as in bearing the weight of," or it can mean "to shelter from above." The latter is the most common meaning and is likely what Paul had in mind in this verse.

Love Is a Retreat That Shelters From the Storms of Life

Love is like a roof over our head that protects us from exposure, ridicule, or harm. In the previous lesson, we discussed the sin of gossip.

Love will shelter a person from the damage of gossip by not participating as a speaker or listener. Even if a person has failed or sinned, love never speaks ill of that person because love covers a multitude of sins (1 Peter 4:8). Spouses should never speak ill of one another; children should never speak ill of their parents; friends should never speak ill of each other.

Love shelters people from damaging words. Love in Christ "bears" all things, while life in the world "bares" all things. Tabloid magazines exist to capitalize on the failings and fallings of famous people. And they wouldn't stay in business unless lots of people were buying those magazines to read the stories. I hope you are not one of them.

When Peter said that love "will cover a multitude of sins," he meant that love is a place to retreat, a place to find shelter from the storms of life.

Love Is a Relationship That Sympathizes With the Sorrows of Life

Love not only shelters, it identifies—it sympathizes and empathizes. To use modern terminology, love "feels the pain" of those who are covered by it. Jesus loved us when He bore our griefs and sorrows and was wounded, bruised, and chastised for us (Isaiah 53:4-5). It is that reality that is the heart of the Christian Gospel: Christ taking our sins upon Himself.

When we love someone, we will enter into the hard places in his or her life and shoulder their burdens for them and with them. We don't stand apart and watch another person suffer. We enter in and pay the price necessary for their well-being.

Love Is a Response That Submits to the Slights of Life

When we are injured, slighted, or not treated properly in life, we can "bear" those insults if we have love. Love is strong in its silence—its ability to endure without fighting back and responding harshly when we are wronged.

Years ago our church needed to hire a new minister of worship, and I had nominated a man that the staff and I felt was an excellent candidate for that position. In our church, the congregation has the responsibility to confirm (or not) these kinds of staff appointments, and when we presented this man's name to the congregation they, by their vote, said, "No." I had never experienced anything like that in ministry before where, as a leader, my recommendation on a weighty issue was rejected by the church. After a period of much discussion within our church staff and family, he was presented to the congregation a second time—and rejected again. So I had the unpleasant task of telling this man, who was a friend I loved very much, that he had been rejected twice by the church.

What I learned during that difficult time was to bear something that made no sense to me at the time, to believe God was doing something bigger than what I could see. I told our congregation, after the second "No" vote, "I want you to know I am not angry. I want you to know that I am disappointed. But I also want you to know that if God doesn't want us to have this man, He must have somebody very special for us." A friend told me later, "I think that's when you *really* became our pastor." The fact that I didn't get angry or retaliate communicated to the church that I loved them—that my love for them was bigger than a decision about an addition to the staff.

The lesson I learned from that experience is that we have to be hurt in order to learn to "bear all things" in love.

The Possibility of Love

If love protects, it also sees the possibility in all things. That doesn't mean a loving person is a gullible person who will believe anything. It means we believe those things that are consistent with what Paul said about love in 1 Corinthians 13:6: Love "rejoices in the truth." If someone has failed or fallen, love believes that person can recover by the grace of God and be restored. Love isn't cynical or pessimistic, but has a positive, faith perspective on life. Love believes the best about people, waiting until a negative report or suspicion is confirmed before drawing conclusions.

Nathaniel Hawthorne was a clerk in the New York City customs department until he was fired for inefficiency. He went home dejected and broken, wondering what he would do. His wife brought a pen and a piece of paper and put it down on the table and said, "Now, Nathaniel, you can do what you always wanted to do. You can write." And so he wrote *The House of the Seven Gables,* then *The Scarlet Letter,* then a string of novels and short stories that made him one of America's most famous authors.

Nathaniel Hawthorne's wife believed all things when she believed in her husband's ability. Upon his death, she said, "I have an eternity, thank God, in which to know him more and more."[1]

How wonderful to have someone in your life whose love translates into a belief in you!

When my choice for a worship leader was not accepted by the majority of our church, I learned one afternoon that a group of people from the church was coming to that evening's business meeting to ask for my resignation. I went into my office and began to weep, and my wife came and put her arms around me and said, "Honey, I'm not worried about this. Never. God will always use you. I believe in you. You don't have to worry. Wherever it is that we go, we're together."

As it turned out, the people didn't come to the meeting; and I'm still at the church. But knowing my wife was beside me, believing in me, gave me the courage to face whatever might come. Everybody needs someone who believes in them—who "believes all things."

People who believe all things . . .

1. Are not suspicious.
2. Believe people are innocent until proven guilty.
3. Don't jump to negative conclusions.
4. Take the best view or interpretation of the facts.
5. Don't assume others have ulterior motives.

There is no situation that divine love within the human cannot face with full hope. That's what love is all about. Love hopes. When love runs out of faith, just hang onto hope.

There are two things hope never does.

Hope Never Allows Facts to Be Forgotten

Hope doesn't deny reality, ignoring the facts of the matter. That would be foolish. Indeed, love-based hope lives in the presence of facts and reality and remains focused on God and His ability instead of man's limited ability.

Jesus never failed to impart hope to people in spite of their difficult circumstances. The Samaritan woman, the woman taken in adultery, the thief on the cross—all were helped and given reason to hope. Even in His parables, hope was a theme: the prodigal son, the lost sheep and coin, and other parables had a theme of hope. Jesus didn't deny reality or the facts. He used them as a way to direct and define hope in that particular situation. Even Jesus, "for the joy that was set before Him endured the cross, despising the shame" (Hebrews 12:2). Jesus had hope in the midst of His own persecution and crucifixion.

Someone has written, "Love does not hope all things by juggling the evidence of the senses. It does not try to convince itself that the thief is honest or the prostitute is pure or the worldly person heavenly minded. But love grapples to its soul with the fact that every man was made for honesty, and purity, and the heavenly vision; and where it cannot find room for its faith in the sad realities of the hour, love slips its hand into the hand of hope and carries its faith onward to the holy arena of good and holy possibility." Love hopes even in the midst of hopelessness. When love runs out of faith, it holds on to hope.

Hope Never Allows Failure to Be Final

In the Old Testament we find God never closing the curtain on the nation of Israel regardless of her failures. The book of Judges is a concise example: seven cycles of sin and discipline that Israel experienced, all the while remaining the people of God. Even when God banished Israel and Judah into exile, Romans 9–11 teaches us that God clearly is not finished with Israel. And just as the prophets foretold, Israel has been called back together as a nation in our lifetime to fulfill the promises of God.

Jesus wouldn't allow Peter's failure to be final, nor would Paul allows the Corinthians' many failures to end their future as a church. Love never allows failure to be final.

THE PATIENCE OF LOVE

There are two primary Greek words for patience. Paul used one of them in verse 4, "love suffers long"; and he uses the other in verse 7, "[love] endures all things." The word in verse 7 refers to patience in terms of things rather than people. It was used, for instance, for an army holding its position on the battlefield at all costs. Every hardship was to be endured in order to stand fast and not be moved.

Patience in verse 4 refers to not receiving what is due, while patience in verse 7 refers to receiving what is not due—specifically, unfair treatment. Love stands firm in spite of how it is treated. It bears, believes, hopes—and then endures regardless. *Agape* love is not the stuff of Hollywood sentimentality. It is the real stuff of life in the person who is strong like God. It is love that goes into the trenches, lives in the trenches, and comes out unshaken. It is the love that keeps marriage partners together when all seems lost. It is the love that keeps a parent praying and waiting for a prodigal child to return. And it is the love that refuses to give up on a best friend who is struggling to stay on the path of righteousness.

At the end of 1 Corinthians 13 we read that "the greatest . . . is love" (verse 13). Love is the virtue that bears, believes, hopes, and endures all things. Make sure that it is your greatest virtue—the virtue others see most clearly in you.

Note

1. Julian Hawthorne, *Nathaniel Hawthorne and His Wife, Volume II* (Cambridge: University Press, 1884), Chapter 10.

PERSONAL QUESTIONS

1. What is your usual response when events in life don't go
   as planned?

   a. What is the significance of what Paul is saying in 1
      Corinthians 13:7? Do the actions in this verse describe your
      response to unplanned events?

   b. Who is in control of all things? (Romans 8:28; Ephesians 1:11)
      How can this be a comfort to us in life's unexpected moments?

2. How is seeing the best in people tied to the idea that is expressed
   in 1 Corinthians 13:6? Is this always easy?

   a. Has anyone ever seen the best in you and encouraged you
      during a dark or hopeless time you were going through?
      How did it leave a mark on your life?

   b. How can you learn to see the best in people and encourage
      them through times that seem hopeless?

   c. How can we be people who "believe all things"? According
      to the lesson, what are five descriptions of people who
      "believe all things"?

      •

      •

•

•

•

d. Does this list describe the way you live? Why or why not?

3. Read Matthew 19:23-30.

   a. What problem did Jesus raise in His teaching in verses 23-24?

   b. What was the disciples' reaction to this teaching? (verse 25)

   c. What was Jesus' solution to this and all hopeless situations? (verse 26)

   d. What hope did Jesus give the disciples with regard to what they had given up for Him? (verses 28-30)

   e. Why can promises from Jesus be the basis of hope (as opposed to promises from other sources)? List examples of promises Christ has kept—both biblically and in your life.

   f. How does "nothing" in Jeremiah 32:17 make "all" in 1 Corinthians 13:7 possible?

GROUP QUESTIONS

1. What is the meaning of the Greek word for "bears" in
   1 Corinthians 13:7?

   a. What are the different ways God's love "bears" life's struggles
      for us?

   b. Discuss some of the ways that love protects us.

   c. What did Jesus teach us by His example of love? (Isaiah 53:4-5)

   d. How is that the reality that is at the heart of the Gospel?

   e. According to the lesson, what must happen in order for us to
      learn to "bear all things" in love? Why?

   f. Explain what "love is strong in its silence" means. Is this
      easy? As a group, discuss examples of how we can do this.

g. What must we comprehend, that is talked about in this lesson, that will help us better understand Paul's words in 1 Corinthians 13:7?

2. Read 1 Peter 2:18-23 and discuss the following questions:

   a. Whom is Peter addressing here? (verse 18) To whom might we apply these words today?

   b. What kind of "bearing up" does Peter suggest might be necessary at times? (verse 19)

   c. How might we interpret the ability to "bear all things" in light of verse 20?

   d. How does verse 20 provide reason to hope in spite of a bad situation?

   e. Who is the ultimate example of "bearing all things," and why? (verses 21-23)

f. How is verse 23 a good example of how to "bear all things"?

3. Why is it a good idea to "believe all things"? (Mark 9:23)

    a. How much faith does it take to accomplish the seemingly
        impossible? (Matthew 17:20)

    b. How can you encourage one another in your faith?

4. Why is Philippians 4:8-9 a good "training passage" for
    1 Corinthians 13:7?

DID YOU KNOW?

Sometimes using Bible paraphrases or expanded translations can provide new insights into the meaning of the original text. For 1 Corinthians 13:7, The Living Bible Classic Edition has, "If you love someone, you will be loyal to him no matter what the cost. You will always believe in him, always expect the best of him, and always stand your ground in defending him." The Message reads, "[Love] puts up with anything, trusts God always, always looks for the best, never looks back, but keeps going to the end." And the Amplified Bible says, "Love bears up under anything and everything that comes, is ever ready to believe the best of every person, its hopes are fadeless under all circumstances, and it endures everything [without weakening]."

LOVE'S POWER OVER TIME

1 Corinthians 13:8

In this lesson we learn why God's love never fails.

OUTLINE

Something is wrong. The Christian community should be manifesting the most enduring love to be found on earth. But marriages fail, scandals surface, and believers argue. Perhaps Christians are not manifesting God's love after all. The Bible says that God's love never fails—never.

   I. Love Never Fails Because God Never Fails—and God Is Love

  II. Love Never Fails Because Christ Never Fails—and Christ Is Love

 III. Love Never Fails When It Is God's Love

First Corinthians is a letter written to what was, sadly, a carnal church. They were relatively young in the Lord, had no New Testament to use as a source of guidance and instruction, and were dependent on traveling teachers, apostles, and Paul's letters to help them learn about life in the Kingdom of God. They had a long way to go.

The Corinthians were divisive, materialistic, morally lax, and prideful in spiritual matters. The one clear message from the book of 1 Corinthians is that a carnal church, a divided church, a worldly church, an indulging church, a compromising church will never be able to effectively proclaim a spiritual message. God could not use the church at Corinth in the way He wanted to use them because they were filled with selfish motivation.

The purpose for the Corinthian church was to reach the city of Corinth. But there was more of Corinth in the church than the church in Corinth. It is not hard to understand why Paul included a chapter on love in his first letter to the Corinthians. They had become carnal in so many ways that they needed to understand that love is the transforming characteristic of every aspect of the Christian life. Chapter 13 is positioned in between two chapters dealing with spiritual gifts because of how unloving the Corinthians were acting with regard to the gifts. But love is not just for spiritual gifts—it is the defining characteristic of all who follow Christ (John 13:35).

In verse 8 of 1 Corinthians 13, Paul turns from the characteristics of love to the enduring permanence of love in contrast to the temporary nature of spiritual gifts: "Love never fails. But whether there are prophecies, they will fail; whether there are tongues, they will cease; whether there is knowledge, it will vanish away." Paul wants them (and us) to focus on what is most important, that being love.

Not only are spiritual gifts temporary, they are incomplete: "For we know in part and we prophesy in part" (verse 9). We gain only partial knowledge and insight from spiritual gifts in this life, but when Christ comes, we will have knowledge that is complete. We will no longer need gifts that manifest Christ through us for we will have Christ Himself. One poet has written about the permanence of love this way:

When prophecy her tale hath finished,
Knowledge hath withered from the trembling tongue,
Love shall survive and love be undiminished,
Love be imperishable, love be young.[1]

Paul is saying that there will never come a time when love will be incapable of performing what it was originally intended to accomplish. It is the one power in this life that is self-generating. It is the one reality in time that goes into eternity unchanged. Love will never need to be transformed into something better because love is the best. It can't be improved. Because it is eternal—heaven will be filled with God's love forever—it is already complete.

When Paul says that "love never fails," he uses the Greek verb *pipto,* a word that means "to fall down, collapse, or fall in value." When we look at the examples of how love in this world falls apart and loses its value, it is evident that the world does not love with God's *agape* love since God's love never, ever fails. Even when Christians love with God's love in this life, it comes to an end when parents pass away or we lose other loved ones in an untimely manner. But that does not mean God's love has failed, for it is eternal. The human object of our love may have passed away, but not love itself.

Another poet has written it this way:

When the last day is ended,
And the nights are through;
When the last sun is buried
In its grave of blue;
When the stars are quenched as candles
And the seas no longer fret,
When the winds unlearn their cunning,
And the storms forget;
When the last lip is palsied,
And the last prayer said,
Love shall reign immortal
While the worlds lie dead.[2]

There are three reasons we can be confident that love will never fail—and they are all based on the character and nature of God Himself.

LOVE NEVER FAILS BECAUSE GOD NEVER FAILS—AND GOD IS LOVE

If we said that love could somehow fail, we would be saying that God could somehow fail because God is love. But the exact opposite is true. Love will never fail because God will never fail. Unlike the other attributes of God mentioned in the Bible (just, true, omnipotent, and others), love is the only attribute specifically equated with God Himself. God is not "loving" in the words of the New Testament—God is love (1 John 4:8, 16). (Note: God certainly is a loving God—I am here only pointing out the specific, singular statement in Scripture that "God is love," something not found with the other attributes.)

The first lie ever told was spoken in the Garden of Eden: Satan told Adam and Eve that God was a liar. He said the first couple would not die if they ate of the tree God had prohibited. And then he told them they could be like God if they did eat. But if anyone wants to be like God, they need to love because God is love.

LOVE NEVER FAILS BECAUSE CHRIST NEVER FAILS—AND CHRIST IS LOVE

The home of love is heaven, but love came to earth in the person of Jesus Christ. To get a human picture of what it means for love never to fail, we need only to look at Jesus—the only human ever to live on earth and live a perfect, unfailing life. Jesus was the personification of *agape* love.

John 13:1 says that "having loved His own who were in the world, [Jesus] loved them to the end." "The end" is *telos* — the absolute limit. Jesus loved His disciples with everything He had, leaving nothing out. That love, Paul says in Ephesians 3:17-19, "passes knowledge." It is almost impossible for us to comprehend the extent of the love of Christ, yet Paul prayed that the Ephesians would get some grasp of it.

It is not hard to see Christ's love in His interactions with those who needed His help—in His love for Peter who had betrayed Him, in forgiving those who had crucified Him, and in dying a cruel death for the ones whose sins put Him on the cross. His love is always love to the uttermost, love to the fullest. The great hymn writer, Isaac Watts, captured that love when he wrote,

See from His head, His hands, His feet,
Sorrow and love flow mingled down.
Did e'er such love and sorrow meet?
Or thorns compose so rich a crown?

LOVE NEVER FAILS WHEN IT IS GOD'S LOVE

If the Father's love and Christ's love never fail, how can I get that quality of love in my life as a Christian? The answer is, when it is "poured out in our hearts by the Holy Spirit" (Romans 5:5).

Human love can't meet the tests of 1 Corinthians 13. Love produced by human striving may be commendable in terms of desire and effort, but it can never be the perfect love of God that Paul exhorts us to manifest. All we have to do is look at the results of human love in the world. It is failing all around us.

Love is the fruit (manifestation) of the Spirit (Galatians 5:22). When the Spirit comes to dwell within us, we have, for the first time, the potential to manifest God's love. Indeed, it is Christ manifesting His love through us (Galatians 2:20). We are given a supernatural ability to love people in situations that we would have found impossible in our own strength. It is only by remaining filled with the Holy Spirit (Ephesians 5:18) that we can remain filled with God's love.

To see what it means for God's love never to fail (1 Corinthians 13:8), here are some examples of things that failed in the New Testament (uses of the verb *pipto):*

- In Matthew 7:27, in the parable Jesus told about the house built on the sand instead of the solid rock, He said the house "fell" *(pipto)* when the winds and flood came against it. A house on an unsure foundation fails, but God's love doesn't fail; God's love doesn't cave in when the storms and pressures of life come against it. Human love will crumble and cave in when the storms of life come against it, but not God's love. Just look at the place where love is supposed to reach its pinnacle—the institution of marriage. The love in Christian marriages fails at a rate just as high as in non-Christian marriages! Without judging the circumstances of anyone's marriage, there is an inconsistency here. Christian love is failing all around us, but God's love never fails.

- In 1 Peter 1:24-25, Peter quotes a passage from Isaiah 40:6 about how flowers fall away in contrast to the permanency of the Word of God. A variant of *pipto*, *ekpipto*, is used—a word that means "to fall away, fall off, or run aground." Just as God's love doesn't cave in when storms come, neither does it fade away with the heat of the sun. A flower in the scorching sun eventually dies. Even in its normal lifespan, a flower doesn't last forever but fades with time. In marriages, love often just fades over time rather than dying from one specific event. But God's love doesn't.

- Acts 27 tells the story of Paul being shipwrecked in the Mediterranean, and verse 29 refers to the ship being "run aground on the rocks." Again, there's the word *ekpipto*— run aground (also in verses 26 and 32). There is no pressure great enough to drive God's love onto the rocks and shoals of life and cause it to run aground. We hear of marriages today that are "on the rocks," but not God's love.

We will not find God's *agape* love in the entertainment we find on television or in the movies today. And yet Christians watch the world's versions of love played out over and over, thinking it has no impact on their thinking. We think that because we don't watch pornography, we are safe. Not true! If we are watching anything that is in conflict with God's never-failing *agape* love, we run the risk of imitating it in our life.

The J. B. Phillips translation of the New Testament translates 1 Corinthians 13:8 this way: "[Love] can outlast anything. It is, in fact, the one thing that still stands when all else has fallen." I've known older couples for whom this is true. Physically, they are weak and have lost their youthful appearance. Perhaps they are limited by physical ailments. Yet they remain deeply committed to one another because of *agape* love—the kind of love that can outlast anything. And that's not natural; it's supernatural.

I remember friends of my parents when I was very young— they had a completely mentally incapacitated daughter. But they loved her until the day she died at 21. She had never responded to their love at all, but that didn't matter. They just poured out their love on her.

A pastor I served with when I went into the ministry had a young son born with significant physical problems. Every night the mother did very painful physical therapy with her son that allowed him to grow up with a degree of physical normalcy. The parents were repaid years later for their love by seeing their son's picture on the front page of the newspaper as being part of a gang that robbed a local bank. But they continued to love him as they worked through the consequences of his bad choices.

These are examples of the kind of love that can only come from God, the kind of love that never fails in spite of the winds and storms, blazing sun, or shoals and rocks that it encounters. Every Christian should pray the prayer written by Amy Carmichael, the selfless missionary to India:

> Mender of broken reeds,
> O patient lover,
> 'Tis love my brother needs.
> Make me a lover.
> That this poor reed may be
> Mended and tuned for Thee;
> O Lord, of even me,
> Make a true lover.
>
> Kindler of smoking flax,
> O fervent Lover,
> Give what Thy servant lacks,
> Make me a lover.
> That this poor flax may be
> Quickened, a flame for Thee;
> O Lord, of even me,
> Make a true lover.[3]

If we are to be "true lovers," we will have to have the love of Him who is truth itself. God's love never fails because He is love. Neither will ours if His love is in us.

Notes

1. Frederic W. H. Myers, *Saint Paul* (London: MacMillan and Co, 1887), 29.

2. Anonymous. Quoted in J. Sidlow Baxter, *Baxter's Explore the Book* (Grand Rapids: Zondervan, 1987), 34.

3. Amy Carmichael, *Mountain Breezes* (Christian Literature Crusade, 1999), 247.

1. Read 1 John 4:7-21.

   a. What reason does John provide for why we should love one another? (verse 7)

   b. What characteristic should define those who claim to know God? (verse 7) Does this characteristic define you?

   c. What is the difference between love being "of God" and God being love? (verses 7-8) Does one flow from the other?

   d. What can we conclude about a person who claims to know God but is not a loving person? (verse 8)

   e. What does verse 8 say about the value of love? How much value do you place on love in your life?

   f. What is the evidence that God has taken up residence in our life? (verse 12)

   g. How do we know that God lives in us? (verse 13; Romans 5:5)

h. Why is verse 14 so important to believers who did not see Jesus personally? How can this verse be an encouragement to you?

i. What is the connection between believing that Jesus is the Son of God and knowing the love of God? (verse 15)

j. In your own words, write down the explanation of the union between God's love and our love, between God in us and us in God. Why does an unloving act or attitude destroy that union? (verse 16)

k. Why does knowing God's love take away fear of judgment? (verse 17)

l. If someone fears death and judgment, what does that say about their knowledge of God's love? (verse 18)

m. Why do we love God? (verse 19)

n. Answer John's question in verse 20. How can this verse be a conviction throughout your life?

1. Discuss what 1 Corinthians 13:8 says about the power of love.

   a. Although the Corinthian church was a young church, with no New Testament to go by, can our churches still relate to the issues that they were going through?

   b. The lesson says, "There was more of Corinth in the church than the church in Corinth." Is the same true for our nation?

   c. How does this affect the purpose of the Church to reach the world?

   d. What is the defining characteristic of all who follow Christ? (John 13:35) Do you think that 1 Corinthians 13 is as applicable to our churches as it was to those in Corinth?

2. Discuss the difference between love and the other spiritual gifts. What makes love so unparalleled?

   a. How is love different from the other attributes of God? Why is this important?

   b. What is the difference between the human object of our love and love itself? How is this related to *agape*?

   c. Because of its relation to God, why will love never fail?

   d. Discuss the differences between human love and God's love. What are some examples of God's love reflected through people? Share some stories of people who may have affected you with their love.

e. How can we reflect God's love to others?

3. Read 1 John 4:7-21 and discuss the following questions.

   a. What can we conclude about a person who claims to know God but is not a loving person? (verse 8) How can this be convicting to all Christians?

   b. How did God manifest His love "toward us"? (verse 9) In light of this, how much should we be willing to sacrifice for others?

DID YOU KNOW?

The word *agape* in the New Testament is a well-known word, standing for God's sacrificial and never-ending love. But there is a word that parallels it in the Old Testament—not exactly, but closely: *hesed. Hesed* is rendered by several different English words depending on context: mercy, kindness, love, or everlasting love. But at the root of its meaning is the idea of "loyal love" (close to "everlasting love"). It is the love that God established between Himself and Israel, a covenant love not dependent on Israel's behavior but on God's choosing, the love that would keep Israel as the apple of His eye forever (Jeremiah 31:33-34). Whether *hesed* or *agape*, God's love never fails.

THE FINAL PRIORITY: PURSUE LOVE

1 Corinthians 13

*In this lesson we learn the human
and divine parts of restoring agape love.*

OUTLINE

Counseling rooms and pastors' offices are filled with people who say, "I've fallen out of love." In order for feelings of love to return, two things are needed: human obedience to the command to love and divine enablement to be able to love. Both are required for the return of *agape* love.

I. **The Spirit-Given Gift**

II. **The Spirit-Given Command**

I t happens everywhere—everywhere there's a piano, at least. You've heard it a million times. In fact, you've probably played it even if you can't play the piano. Within five seconds several younger members of the group are going to make a mad dash for the door, racing to see who can get to that empty space on the piano bench to add the right hand element to the age-old classic, "Heart and Soul."

"Heart and Soul" is a simple love song with lyrics that express what all lovers have felt. Some of the lyrics are "Heart and soul, I fell in love with you, heart and soul, the way a fool would do, madly." The song is full of the lyrics of love: love, adore, madly, and on and on. But the key to the meaning of the song, and the meaning of love, is the phrase "heart and soul."

When we love—really, truly love—we love with our whole self, our entire being. There's no holding back. Isn't that how you loved when you first met the love of your life? (And hopefully still do!) There was nothing you wouldn't have done for that person. Your heart, soul, time, money, abilities—you devoted it all to the love of your life. Your heart and your whole being were a visible expression of your love.

It was Moses who told the second generation of Israelites, as they were about to cross over the Jordan to claim Canaan as their Promised Land, that they must "love the Lord your God with all your heart, with all your soul, and with all your strength" (Deuteronomy 6:5).

The Hebrew language used words like *heart, soul,* and *strength* as synonyms more times than not. He was saying, "Love God with your whole being, all that you are. Don't hold back anything. If you do, you won't be loving God or anyone else."

When Jesus was asked, "Which is the first commandment of all?" He didn't quote the first of the Ten Commandments. He quoted Moses from Deuteronomy 6:4-5: "And you shall love the Lord your God with all your heart, with all your soul, with all your mind, and with all your strength" (Mark 12:30). See the fourth human dimension Jesus' added to Moses' three? Jesus added the "mind" —that we should love God with all our mental faculties as well, further expanding the totality of our love life toward God.

But then Jesus said, "This is the first commandment. And the second, like it, is this: 'You shall love your neighbor as yourself'" (verses 30-31).

What is Jesus saying with these two commandments? That loving God is the foundation for all other loves, that loving God must precede our love for others (our neighbor, whether spouse, child, friend, or stranger). Therefore, Jesus' first and second commandments are more than a priority list in a theological sense. They are a priority list practically speaking as well. We must love God—have an understanding of His love in Christ and have embraced that love as evidenced by our love for Him—if we are going to be able to love others.

Think about how you love God and see if it is reflected in how you love others:

- With your heart: unconditionally.
- With your soul: passionately.
- With your mind: willfully.
- With your strength: continually.

Loving God with "heart and whole" is the foundation of all other loves.

This study guide has focused on the greatest treatise on love ever written—1 Corinthians 13. Three paragraphs, 280 words—but the most profound word on the subject of love in all the world's literature. It's about love that transcends prophecy and knowledge and understanding; love that edifies instead of puffing up one with pride; love that is the foundation of all other ministry and achievement for God; love that transcends good works, benevolence, and a martyr's death. Paul wrote that if we have the faith, the good works, and the courage to face death as a martyr but don't have love, we don't have anything!

At least 55 times in the New Testament, Christians are commanded to love. That's what tells us love is a command and a responsibility, not a feeling or an option. I've talked with many people over the years who have told me they no longer "feel anything" for the person to whom they're married. The answer to that person is, "So you've decided to disobey the Lord? To go back on your promise to love?" We must recommit ourselves to the biblical proposition that love is a responsibility, not a feeling. And that not to love is disobedience. When we obey God by loving, the feelings follow. But when we make feelings the priority, it is far too easy to "fall out of love."

In this concluding lesson, I want to take up this question of loving in obedience to the Lord—how, exactly, do we do it?

THE SPIRIT-GIVEN GIFT

In Galatians 5:22-23, Paul listed the characteristics of the Holy Spirit in the life of a believer—what he called "the fruit of the Spirit." There is a wonderful correlation between the characteristics of love in 1 Corinthians 13 and the fruit of the Spirit. When we compare these two passages, we see both the human and the divine role in manifesting love in our life. Our responsibility, the human role, is in 1 Corinthians 13; and the divine role, fulfilled by the Holy Spirit, is in Galatians 5. While love is our commanded responsibility, the fact is that true, *agape* love is the fruit of God alone. As we have already studied in these lessons, God is love; and when He lives in us, we can manifest His love. We can't produce it by our flesh.

But while love is produced in us by God, it is our responsibility to manifest that love by our choices. If that were not true, Paul would not have been writing to the Corinthian believers about their lack of love. It was their responsibility to obey God and allow His love to be manifested through their lives. (That's why Paul told them in 1 Corinthians 14:1 to "pursue love.") We don't just sit around and wait for God to "zap" us with a loving feeling from heaven. Love is the fruit of the Spirit (Galatians 5:22). As we obey the command to be filled with the Spirit (Ephesians 5:18), that fruit will be manifested in our life.

- Joy: the strength of love. The second fruit of the Spirit in Galatians 5:22 is joy, and in 1 Corinthians 13:6, Paul tells us to rejoice in the truth. Joy is a characteristic of the Kingdom of God (Romans 14:17). Paul wrote a letter with joy mentioned throughout (Philippians)—from prison! While the Holy Spirit produces joy, it is our responsibility to manifest it.

- Peace: the security of love. Following joy in Galatians 5:22, Paul mentions peace; and in the love chapter, he says that love "thinks no evil" (verse 5). There can be no peace when we keep lists of the wrongs committed against us.

- Longsuffering: the stability of love. The third fruit after love that Paul mentions is "longsuffering"—exactly what he says love is in 1 Corinthians 13:4. Patience is our responsibility, but is produced by the Spirit.

- Kindness: the sobriety of love. Paul wrote in 1 Corinthians 13:4 that "love . . . is kind" and in verse 5 that "[love] does not behave rudely." If anyone is going to love, it will take the Spirit to manifest kindness.

- Goodness: the simplicity of love. Paul's mention of goodness in Galatians 5 could be compared to his saying that "love does not parade itself, is not puffed up" in 1 Corinthians 13:4. It is human nature to be proud; it is the nature of the Spirit to produce humility and goodness.

- Faith: the surety of love. The next part of the fruit of the Spirit is faithfulness which Paul covers in 1 Corinthians 13:7: "[Love] bears all things, believes all things, hopes all things, endures all things." Who could do "all" those things without the empowering of the Spirit?

- Gentleness: the selflessness of love. Gentleness, or meekness, is what Paul wrote about in 1 Corinthians 13 when he said, "[Love] does not behave rudely, does not seek its own" (verse 5).

- Self-control: the selflessness of love. "Love does not envy," Paul wrote in 1 Corinthians 13:4. It takes the supernatural work of the Spirit to be content in a world that encourages us to be discontent.

Only the Holy Spirit makes it possible for us to carry out the command to love.

THE SPIRIT-GIVEN COMMAND

Besides the command to love, there are Scriptures that command us to manifest all the rest of the fruit of the Spirit as well:

- Joy. "Rejoice in the Lord always" (Philippians 4:4).
- Peace. "Pursue peace with all people" (Hebrews 12:14).
- Longsuffering. "Be patient with all" (1 Thessalonians 5:14).
- Kindness. "And be kind to one another" (Ephesians 4:32).
- Goodness. "We are . . . created in Christ Jesus for good works" (Ephesians 2:10).
- Faithfulness. "Moreover it is required . . . that one be found faithful" (1 Corinthians 4:2).
- Gentleness. "Remind them to be . . . gentle" (Titus 3:1-2).
- Self-control. "And everyone who competes for the prize is temperate in all things" (1 Corinthians 9:25).

I know only one way to live the life of love Paul describes in 1 Corinthians 13: Be obedient to the commands of God—regardless of feelings. When we fail to love because of our feelings, we are disobeying the commands of God. Husbands and wives are expected, before God, to love one another as a choice, an act of the will. Feelings are to be expected, and they are good. But they are not the command of God. Positive emotional feelings are the result, the by-product, of living in obedience to God.

The concept of love in the world today is that we love "because of what you can do for me." God's idea of love is to love "in spite of what you don't do for me." It doesn't matter if the person we love never responds. Our commitment and responsibility is to love in spite of that lack of response. That's how Pat Williams loved his wife for month after month, attempting to rekindle the love between them. There was no response for the longest time, but he continued to love his wife until the spark became a flame and the passion of their love was restored. She could not refuse the selfless, *agape* love of her husband.

When I spoke at a conference on *agape* love, a father approached me to talk about his nineteen-year-old son who had been rebelling the last several years. The father said he realized that he, not the son, was the problem. He said he had not loved his son with *agape* love—spending the time with him that he deserved and loving him "in spite of." But he said he intended to start. He told me later that, after we talked, he went to the phone and called his son at home to ask for his forgiveness and to commit himself to being the kind of father his son needed. They both wept together as the Holy Spirit provided a new breakthrough in their relationship.

Love can be rekindled, individually or corporately. Jesus Christ spoke to the church at Ephesus about how they had lost their first love (Revelation 2:1-6). And what did He tell them to do? "Remember therefore from where you have fallen; repent and do the first works" (verse 5). And that's what we have to do as well—remember what love was like when it first blossomed and what we did in response. Then go back and do those sacrificial acts again.

Whether it is a husband needing to love his wife, a wife her husband, a parent his or her child, a church its own members—love can be rekindled if we will "repent and do the first works" again. If we simply wait for the feelings to return, they won't—and neither will love. The feelings were there in the first place because of acts of love you performed. And you must return to those same acts in order for the feelings to return.

I can hear you thinking, "That won't work for me." On the authority of God's Word, the God who is love, I can assure you that it will.

PERSONAL QUESTIONS

1. Read Ecclesiastes 5:1-7 in terms of the vows to love that are made in the Christian marriage ceremony.

   a. Verses 1-2 refer to vows made "before God." In what sense is that true of Christian marriage vows? What is the importance of promises made before the Lord?

   b. Why are the warnings of verse 2 particularly relevant for marriage? When you commit to someone before God, how much thought and prayer should go into that decision?

   c. What obligation do those who make marriage vows before "God and these witnesses" take upon themselves? (verse 4)

   d. What is the warning in verse 5? To what should a bride and groom be utterly committed before they enter into their vows? (Genesis 2:24; Matthew 19:6)

   e. What does your "flesh" do when it doesn't keep vows that are made? (verse 6)

   f. Why does it not work to say, "Sorry, I made a mistake"? (verses 2, 6)

   g. What is God's response to those who make vows and then break them? (verses 4, 6)

h. Why should the words "I love you" (in a marriage sense) be spoken carefully? (Proverbs 20:25)

i. How can extensive premarital counseling serve to prevent rash vow-making?

j. What hope is there for those who have made marriage vows and then broken them? (Psalm 32:5; Proverbs 28:13; 1 John 1:9)

2. What are some of the characteristics of *agape* love?

a. Where can you get *agape* love? How? What is its source?

b. Is sacrificial, *agape* love a choice or a feeling? What can happen if you aren't fully committed to manifesting *agape* love in your relationships?

c. Are there any relationships in your life that may be failing? How can they be rekindled?

d. Why is it important to distinguish the fact that love is "a command and a responsibility, not a feeling or an option"?

e. When it comes to manifesting love, why can we not rely solely on our feelings?

1. List the fruit of the Spirit (Galatians 5:22-23) and discuss their correlation with the characteristics of love in 1 Corinthians 13.

   ●

   ●

   ●

   ●

   ●

   ●

   ●

   ●

   a. What is the human role in manifesting love in our life? (1 Corinthians 13)

b. What is the divine role in manifesting love in our life? (Galatians 5:22-23)

c. How do we love in obedience to the Lord?

d. If we view loving others as a commandment from God (John 15:12) instead of a suggestion, how will that change the way we treat people?

e. Discuss the difference between the definition of love in our culture and the kind of love God commands us to have.

2. What was the "new commandment" Jesus gave His disciples in John 13:34?

a. Why did He single out this one behavior? Of what is love the primary evidence? (John 13:35)

b. How "new" was this commandment? (Leviticus 19:18) Was it the commandment that was new or the way it was to be used as a marker for the community of Jesus' disciples?

3. What impact does a lack of love have in terms of identifying the Christian community?

4. How can your group work on reflecting God's love to those in the community around you?

5. What is the measure for how we are to love one another? (John 13:34) Expand on ways in which we can do that.

DID YOU KNOW?

In biblical theology, there is sometimes tension between God's responsibility and man's responsibility, a tension theologians refer to as an antinomy (*anti* = against, *nomos* = law). An antinomy is something that is contrary to law or reason, such as God's sovereignty and man's responsibility, both of which are true. They are like parallel halves of a railroad track that run beside each other, both necessary, but never resolving into a single entity. The human mind doesn't like to hold two contradictory but equally true ideas in tension; but when it comes to love, that is what we must do: our responsibility, but impossible without God's empowering.

NOTES

NOTES

NOTES

NOTES

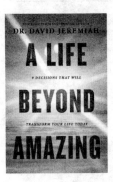

A Life Beyond Amazing

Love, joy, peace, endurance, humility—these are the traits Christ exhibited continually while on earth. Christ left us His Spirit after He ascended to heaven so that we might display these traits—"the fruit of the Spirit"—as well. In *A Life Beyond Amazing: 9 Decisions That Will Transform Your Life Today*, Dr. David Jeremiah explores the nine traits of the Spirit-filled life and explains that we can live an extraordinary life here on earth if we abide in Christ.

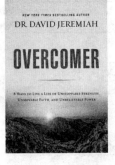

Overcomer

In *Overcomer: Eight Ways to Live a Life of Unstoppable Strength, Unmovable Faith, and Unbelievable Power!* Dr. David Jeremiah explores Paul's description of spiritual armor, explaining what it means for Christians to overcome in this world filled with sin and evil. He explains how, when we put on Christ, we have everything we need to stand victorious and overcome!

Hope—An Anchor For Life

God's hope forges an anchor for the soul, steadfast and sure. It's a real, guaranteed hope that dispels discouragement and inspires joy and confidence. In *Hope—An Anchor for Life*, Dr. David Jeremiah takes you on a tour of the most hopeful passages of Scripture and focuses on practical topics that will encourage and bless you in your walk with God.

Count It All Joy

The apostle Paul's most personal letter was sent to the Christians of Philippi. This intimate and loving epistle was written to believers who lived in the shadow of the Roman tyrant, Nero. Paul was in a Roman prison, facing an uncertain future, and yet he wrote of the importance of joy. In *Count It All Joy*, Dr. David Jeremiah leads you through the book of Philippians so that you too can experience the joy of the Lord in your daily life.

Each of these resources was created from a teaching series by Dr. David Jeremiah. Contact Turning Point for more information about correlating materials.

For pricing information and ordering, contact us at

P.O. Box 3838
San Diego, CA 92163
(800) 947-1993
www.DavidJeremiah.org